AS SHE FLASHED HER LIGHT ABOUT SHE SAW THAT SHE
HAD MADE NO MISTAKE.

The Secret of the Old Clock. *Page* 158

" NOT MUCH YOU **DON'T**," HE SNARLED.

The Secret of the Old Clock.   *Page* 131

"WITHOUT AN INSTANT'S HESITATION, SHE HEADED STRAIGHT
FOR THE BUILDING AND DROVE IN."

The Secret of the Old Clock. **Page 30**

"THERE'S A CLOCK IN FRONT OF YOU," ISABEL TOLD HER
POINTEDLY.

The Secret of the Old Clock.   *Frontispiece (Page* 100)

NANCY DREW MYSTERY STORIES

THE SECRET OF THE OLD CLOCK

By
CAROLYN KEENE

AUTHOR OF
NANCY DREW MYSTERY STORIES: THE HIDDEN STAIRCASE
NANCY DREW MYSTERY STORIES: THE BUNGALOW MYSTERY

ILLUSTRATED BY
RUSSELL H. TANDY

WITH AN INTRODUCTION BY
SARA PARETSKY

FACSIMILE EDITION

1991
BEDFORD, MA
APPLEWOOD BOOKS

For further information about these editions, please write:
Applewood Books, Box 365, Bedford, MA 01730.

LIBRARY OF CONGRESS CATALOGING-IN-PUBLICATION DATA
Keene, Carolyn.
     The secret of the old clock / by Carolyn Keene;
illustrated by Russell H. Tandy; with an introduction by
Sara Paretsky. —Facsimile ed.
     p.   cm.   — (Nancy Drew mystery stories)
     Summary: Nancy Drew's keen mind is tested
when she searches for a missing will.
     ISBN 1-55709-155-2
     [1. Mystery and detective stories.]   I. Tandy,
Russell H., ill.   II. Title.   III. Series: Keene, Carolyn.
Nancy Drew mystery stories.

PZ7.K23Seo	1991	91-46735
[Fic]–dc20		CIP
		AC

20 19 18 17 16

PUBLISHER'S NOTE

Applewood Books is pleased to reissue the original Hardy Boys and Nancy Drew books, just as they were originally published—the Hardy Boys in 1927 and Nancy Drew in 1930. In 1959, the books were condensed and rewritten, and since then, the original editions have been out of print.

Much has changed in America since the books were first issued. The modern reader may be delighted with the warmth and exactness of the language, the wholesome innocence of the characters, their engagement with the natural world, or the nonstop action without the use of violence; but just as well, the modern reader may be extremely uncomfortable with the racial and social stereotyping, the roles women play in these books, or the use of phrases or situations which may conjure up some response in the modern reader that was not felt by the reader of the times.

For good or bad, we Americans have changed quite a bit since these books were first issued. Many readers will remember these editions with great affection and will be delighted with their return; others will wonder why we just don't let them disappear. These books are part of our heritage. They are a window on our real past. For that reason, except for the addition of this note and the introduction by Sara Paretsky, we are presenting *The Secret of the Old Clock* unedited and unchanged from its first edition.

Applewood Books
September 1991

Going back to the original Nancy Drew, as Applewood Books has done, is to take a revealing journey into our nation's social history. The books we relished as children dished up some dreadful racial attitudes. Hopefully we have outgrown those views, but we shouldn't forget how pervasive a part of American culture they were for many decades.

At the same time, Nancy Drew offered girls of 1930 an amazing alternative to the career choice of secretary and milliner that other children's books provided. Her enduring popularity probably has no deeper cause than that: little girls need to see a bigger girl act competently and solve problems they keep being told belong to boys. Even though today's children can look at female spies, astronauts, doctors, and other fictional heroes, they still need the girl detective to inspire them.

> "A puncture!" Nancy murmured in disgust. "If that isn't just my luck! Oh, well, I suppose I must fix it myself, because there won't be another car for an hour on this road."
>
> It was not the first time Nancy Drew had changed a tire, but she never relished the task. Rummaging under the seat, she pulled out the tools and quickly jacked up the rear axle. She loosened the lugs ... and tugged at [the tire] ... [T]he huge balloon tire could not be budged. Then, as she gave one mighty tug, it came off and Nancy Drew fell backwards into a sitting posture in the road.
>
> "Well it's off, anyway," she told herself with satisfaction, as she brushed the dirt from her clothing.
> —*The Secret of the Old Clock* (page 107)

What could be more inspiring and appealing? Here's a heroine who is undaunted by car problems, tackles a job she doesn't relish and succeeds at it, and doesn't mind landing in the dirt in her nice clothes.

Nancy Drew made a wonderful antidote to the America of my childhood. When I was four a neighbor boy and I watched a woman drive a panel truck across the University of Kansas campus. "Ladies don't drive trucks," the toddler pronounced in disgust. His mother chortled over his wisdom, repeating it for years after with all the delight of Mrs. Newton recapitulating her son's laws of gravity.

Of course ladies in the fifties did drive trucks, especially in the farm community where I grew up, but we weren't supposed to applaud them. Yet Nancy Drew handled her blue sports car on dangerous roads with unfailing expertise. She spent eight hours on a lake in a stalled boat without panicking or screaming for help, learned to fly so well she awed her instructor, and diagnosed and fixed a flawed distributor when her car misbehaved. To a nation where car mechanics still mock or brush off complaints by women Nancy remains a significant role model.

In my childhood women were supposed to be as ignorant of mathematics as of motors. It's still hard to get young girls to test their analytical powers. But Nancy Drew's thoughts turn immediately to Archimedes when she's locked in a closet; she knows if she can find a lever she can pry open the hinges. She feels some fear in that closet, and — contrary to the monolithic view scholars like to suggest — she expe-

It is easy to poke fun at the girl detective — at her adeptness with Old English and modern French, her intrepidity when locked in closets or towers, buried in mudslides, or threatened by the dastardly. It's easy, too, to lampoon the conscious assumption of WASP superiority in the early books in the series. Government and social status, at least in the early books, rightly belong to "the wise, the rich, and the well," in Alexander Hamilton's phrase.

Of course Peter Wimsey could match Nancy Drew skill for skill, intrepid moment for intrepid moment, and outdoes her in keeping all grace, intelligence, and morality in upper class hands. But maybe we tolerate French, Latin, brandy tasting, professional levels of acrobatics, diving, and piano playing, expertise with swords, guns, automobiles, Scarlatti, sonnet writing, and medicine in a titled Englishman that we scoff at in a Midwestern girl.

The early books in the series were slightly rewritten to modernize them in the late fifties. The most objectionable racial stereotyping was removed. Nancy was aged from sixteen to eighteen. Perhaps in the Depression, a sixteen-year-old who didn't have to go to school and who successfully managed her father's house didn't seem as anomalous as it later became. Perhaps series editors didn't like a sixteen-year-old at the wheel of a roadster. Whatever the reason, Nancy's a little older and she dresses more casually. Her hair changed from gold to titian and back to gold again. She still solves her own problems, though without adult or male interference.

KEEPING NANCY DREW ALIVE

By

SARA PARETSKY

AUTHOR OF
THE V.I. WARSHAWSKI MYSTERY SERIES: BURN MARKS
THE V.I. WARSHAWSKI MYSTERY SERIES: BLOOD SHOT
THE V.I. WARSHAWSKI MYSTERY SERIES: GUARDIAN ANGEL
& OTHERS

MENTION NANCY DREW to any woman between the ages of twenty-five and seventy, and chances are her face will turn dreamy and she'll say, "Nancy Drew! I haven't thought about her for years, but I used to love her." Nancy Drew and her blue roadster have been symbols of freedom for little girls since Grosset & Dunlap first published *The Secret of the Old Clock*, in 1930. With almost two hundred titles in the series, and new adventures arriving at the rate of eighteen a year, it's clear that Nancy's appeal is as strong as ever.

Hardcover sales of Nancy Drew adventures have surpassed Agatha Christie's phenomenal record. Publications from the *Journal of Popular Culture* to the *Wall Street Journal* have pondered the series' popularity without presenting a convincing explanation. At the same time, scholars complain about the pell-mell pace of the adventures and the protected environment in which Nancy lives.

riences remorse. She knows she has only herself to thank that her father thinks she's having a good time at camp and won't look for her for at least a week. What makes her heroic is that she rises above fear and despair and finds herself a lever.

Nancy's lifestyle is just as appealing to girls raised with endless shibboleths. Her mother is dead. Her lawyer-father and his housekeeper treat her opinions with adult respect. They place no restrictions on her comings and goings, because they know she won't behave irresponsibly.

Early in the series Nancy acquired a boyfriend, handsome Ned Nickerson, who flexes his muscles for a college football team. She also has two enduring girlfriends, boyish George Fayne and George's ultra-feminine cousin Bess Marvin. Like Dr. Watson, none of the three is a match for the sleuth, either in ability to figure out clues or in the scope of their skills. And in a reversal of the usual male-female relations in crime fiction, Ned's function is primarily decorative. He also is more attached to Nancy than she to him. Occasionally he brings up the question of marriage, but Nancy refuses to respond; she doesn't want to give up her independent sleuthing life for domesticity.

Little girls today still grow up without a strong sense of themselves as people or of their right to play active roles in adult life. Scholarly studies show that as girls head into their teens they stop trying to succeed for fear of showing up boys. Today, girls emerge from adolescence with a much lower sense of self-esteem than boys. Nancy never minded leaving Ned Nickerson in the dirt; his adoration never flagged for all the times she proved herself smarter and quicker than he.

In parts of the country, the highpoint of a girl's life may be making the cheerleading squad: a Texas mother was charged with attempting murder to guarantee that *summum bonum* to her daughter.

Nancy Drew doesn't lead cheers. She undertakes the heroics that keep others cheering. She is expert in some traditional girlish arts — tap-dancing, for instance. She uses that skill, though, not to become a cheerleader or Miss America, but to tap out Morse code when she's imprisoned.

Nancy's adventures appeal most to girls of ten or eleven. After that they move — is it on or backwards? — to stories where romantic conflict plays a bigger role and where heroines aren't as invincible as the girl detective. They leave the fantasy world of eleven to deal with the hard reality of women's lives.

Of course, girls couldn't really imagine undertaking Nancy's detective adventures. The facts of violent assault are a strong inducement to stay close to home, even if that home has a parent as adoring and considerate as Carson Drew. But it's a wonderful dream, that a girl can get in her blue roadster, steer it down perilous roads, and come home triumphant. Instead of making little girls leave that dream, maybe it's time we changed their reality. Keeping Nancy Drew alive for them can only help.

NANCY DREW MYSTERY STORIES

THE SECRET OF THE OLD CLOCK

BY

CAROLYN KEENE

AUTHOR OF "THE HIDDEN STAIRCASE," "THE
BUNGALOW MYSTERY," ETC.

ILLUSTRATED BY

RUSSELL H. TANDY

NEW YORK
GROSSET & DUNLAP
PUBLISHERS

Made in the United States of America

NANCY DREW
MYSTERY STORIES

By CAROLYN KEENE

12mo. Cloth. Illustrated.

––––––

THE SECRET OF THE OLD CLOCK

THE HIDDEN STAIRCASE

THE BUNGALOW MYSTERY

(Other volumes in preparation)

––––––

GROSSET & DUNLAP, PUBLISHERS, NEW YORK

CONTENTS

Contents

THE SECRET OF THE OLD CLOCK

CHAPTER I

The Lost Will

"It would be a shame if all that money went to the Tophams! They will fly higher than ever!"

Nancy Drew, a pretty girl of sixteen, leaned over the library table and addressed her father who sat reading a newspaper by the study lamp.

"I beg your pardon, Nancy. What were you saying about the Tophams?"

Carson Drew, a noted criminal and mystery-case lawyer, known far and wide for his work as a former district attorney, looked up from his evening paper and smiled indulgently upon his only daughter. Now, as he gave her his respectful attention, he was not particularly concerned with the Richard Topham family but rather with the rich glow of the lamp upon

1

Nancy's curly golden bob. Not at all the sort of head which one expected to indulge in serious thoughts, he told himself.

Mischievously, Nancy reached over and tweaked his ear.

"You weren't paying a bit of attention," she accused him sternly. "I was saying I think it's mean if those snobbish Tophams fall heir to all of Josiah Crowley's fortune. Can't something be done about it?"

Removing his horn-rimmed spectacles and carefully folding the paper, Carson Drew regarded his daughter meditatively.

"I'm afraid not, Nancy. A will is a will, you know."

"But it does seem unfair that *all* the money should go to them. Especially when they never treated Josiah Crowley like a human being!"

"The Tophams were never noted for their charitable dispositions," Carson Drew observed, with a smile. "However, they did give Josiah a home."

"Yes, and everyone knows why! They wanted to work him into leaving all his money to them. And it seems that their scheme worked, too! They treated him like a prince until he made his will in their favor and then they acted as though he were dirt under their feet. Folks said he died just to be rid of their everlasting nagging."

"The Tophams aren't very well liked in our little city, are they?" Mr. Drew commented dryly.

"Who could like them, father? Richard Topham is an old skinflint who made his money by gambling on the stock exchange. And Cora, his wife, is nothing but a vapid social climber. The two girls, Isabel and Ada, are even worse. I went to school with them, and I never saw such stuck-up creatures in all my life. If they fall heir to any more money, this town won't be big enough to hold them!"

In her estimate of the Topham family, Nancy Drew did not exaggerate. Nearly everyone in River Heights shared the opinion that the Tophams were snobbish and arrogant, and the treatment they accorded old Josiah Crowley had aroused a great deal of unfavorable comment.

Nancy had never known Josiah well, but had often seen him on the street and secretly had regarded him as a rather nice but extremely queer sort of individual. His wife had died during the influenza epidemic following the World War, and since that time Crowley had made his home with various relatives. Although well-to-do, he preferred to "visit around."

At first, the Tophams had evidenced no interest in the old man and he had been forced to live with kindly relatives who were scarcely able to have him with them. Crowley appreciated the sacrifice and openly declared that he intended to make his will in their favor.

Then, three years before his death, the Topham family experienced a sudden change of heart. They begged Josiah Crowley to make his home with them, and at last he consented. Presently, rumor had it that the Tophams had induced him to make his will in their favor.

But as time went on and Mr. Crowley, though failing in health, maintained as firm a grip on life as ever, the Tophams treated him unkindly. Although he continued to live with them, it was whispered about that frequently he slipped away to visit his old friends and that he intended to change his will again, cutting the Tophams out entirely.

Then one day Josiah Crowley took to his bed and did not get up. Just before his death he attempted to communicate something to the doctor who attended him, but his words were unintelligible. After the funeral, only one will came to light and, to the surprise of everyone, it gave the entire fortune to the Tophams.

"Father, what do you suppose it was that Mr. Crowley tried to tell the doctor just before he died?" Nancy demanded, after a moment of thought. "Do you imagine he was trying to disclose something about his will?"

"Very likely, Nancy. Probably he intended to leave his money to more deserving relatives. But fate cheated him of the opportunity."

"But isn't it possible that he did make such a will and that he was trying to tell what he had done with it?"

"Yes, that's a possibility of course. Josiah Crowley was rather queer in many ways."

"Perhaps he hid the will somewhere," Nancy suggested thoughtfully.

"If he did, I'm afraid it will never come to light. The Tophams will see to that."

"What do you mean, father?"

"The estate is a considerable one, I understand, Nancy, and the Tophams don't intend that anyone shall get a cent of it. It's my private opinion that they will take care that a second will is never found."

"Do you mean that if they discovered the will they would destroy it?"

"Well, I'm not making any accusations, Nancy. But I do know that Richard Topham is shrewd, and he isn't noted for his honesty."

"Can't the present will be broken?"

"I doubt it. While I haven't gone into the case, I am of the opinion that the Tophams have a legal right to the fortune. It would cost considerable to contest the will, and so far as I know the other relatives are in poverty. They have filed a claim, declaring that a later will was made in their favor, but I doubt that the matter will ever go further.''

"But the Tophams don't deserve the fortune, father. It doesn't seem fair.''

"No, it isn't fair. But it is legal, and I'm afraid nothing can be done about it. There were two girls who live somewhere on the River Road that were great pets of Crowley's when they were children. It seems to me that they should have had something. And there are a number of relatives who really deserve a portion of the fortune.''

Nancy nodded thoughtfully and relapsed into silence while she digested the facts of the case. From her father she had acquired the habit of thinking things through to their logical conclusion. Frequently, Carson Drew had assured her that she went at a thing "like a detective." Certainly she had a naturally clever mind and took more than an ordinary interest in strange or baffling cases.

Carson Drew, a widower, showered a great deal of affection upon his daughter; it was his secret boast that he had taught her to think for herself and to think logically. Since he knew that Nancy could be trusted with confidential information, he frequently discussed his interesting cases with her.

A number of times Nancy had been present at interviews which her father had had with noted detectives who desired his aid in solving perplexing mysteries, and those occasions stood out as red letter days for her.

There was something about a mystery which aroused Nancy's interest, and she was never content until it was solved. More than once her father had found her suggestions, or "intuitions" as he called them, extremely helpful.

For a reason which she could not understand, the Crowley case had attracted Nancy's attention, although it had not fallen into her father's hands. She had a certain feeling that a mystery lurked behind it.

"Father, do you believe Josiah Crowley ever made a second will?" Nancy demanded suddenly.

"You're a regular lawyer, the way you cross-examine me," Carson Drew protested, but with evident enjoyment. "To tell you the truth, I don't know whether he ever made a second will or not. All I do know is that— but perhaps I shouldn't mention it since my information is not very definite."

"Go on!" Nancy commanded impatiently. "You're trying to tease me!"

"Well, I do remember that one day nearly a year ago I was standing in the First National Bank when Crowley came in with Henry Rolsted."

"Not the attorney who specializes in wills and legal documents?"

"Yes. Well, as I was saying, they came into the bank together. I had no intention of listening to their conversation, but I couldn't help but hear that they were discussing a will. Crowley made an appointment to call at Rolsted's office the following day."

"That looks as though Mr. Crowley had made up his mind to write a new will, doesn't it?"

"That was the thought which passed through my mind at the time."

"You say you overheard the conversation nearly a year ago," Nancy mused. "That was nearly two years after Mr. Crowley had made the will in favor of the Tophams, wasn't it?"

"Yes. It's likely Crowley had made up his mind to change the will. I suspect he intended to cut the Tophams out, but whether or not he did, I have no way of knowing."

"Mr. Rolsted is an old friend of yours, isn't he?"

"He is. An old friend and an old college classmate."

"Then why don't you ask him if he ever drew up a will for Mr. Crowley?"

"That's a rather delicate question to ask, young lady. He may tell me it's none of my business."

"You know he won't. You're such a noted

attorney that other lawyers feel flattered when you take an interest in their cases. Will you do it? Please!''

"I can't promise to blunder into his office and demand the information. Why this sudden interest in the case, Nancy?"

"Oh, I don't know. A mystery always interests me, I guess, and it does seem to me that someone ought to help those poor relatives."

"You take after your old dad, I am afraid. But I'm curious to know what mystery you have discovered."

"If a will is missing, isn't that a mystery?"

"If it is actually missing—yes. But it's possible that if Crowley ever wrote the will he changed his mind and destroyed it. He was subject to sudden whims, you know."

"Anyhow, I'd like to learn more about the case if I can. Will you talk with Mr. Rolsted?"

"You are persistent, Nancy," and Mr. Drew smiled. "Well, I suppose I could invite him to take luncheon with me to-morrow——"

"Oh, please do," Nancy interrupted eagerly. "That would be a splendid opportunity to find out everything he knows about the will."

"All right, I'll try to do it. But I warn you not to expect startling news." Carson Drew glanced at his watch. "Why, it's nearly midnight, Nancy. We've been discussing this case for over an hour. Better run off to bed now and forget the Tophams."

"All right," Nancy agreed somewhat reluctantly. "Don't forget your promise tomorrow at luncheon!"

Long after his daughter had retired, Carson Drew sat by the fire. At last he, too, arose.

"It wouldn't surprise me if Nancy has stumbled upon a real mystery," he told himself, as he snapped out the electric light and turned toward the stairway. "Perhaps I shouldn't encourage her to dig into it, but after all it's in a good cause!"

CHAPTER II

A Chance Meeting

"Don't forget your luncheon engagement with Mr. Rolsted," Nancy Drew reminded her father the next morning at the breakfast table.

"I'll telephone him the first thing after I reach my office," Carson Drew promised. "But again I warn you not to anticipate startling news."

"I won't, father," Nancy laughed. "But if I should happen to learn something which has a bearing on the missing will, I won't be exactly disappointed."

"What are your plans for the day, Nancy?"

"Oh, nothing special. I thought I would do a little shopping this morning. And I am invited to a party one of the girls is giving in the afternoon."

"Then you are too busy to take luncheon with me."

"Oh, father, you know I've just been dying for an invitation!" Nancy declared, her eyes dancing. "I'm so anxious to learn something about that will!"

"All right, if you have time, drop in at my office about twelve-thirty. Mr. Rolsted may not accept my invitation, but if he does, we'll try to find out something about Josiah Crowley. Of course I don't need to warn you not to appear too eager for information."

"I'll let you do all the talking," Nancy told him. "I'll just keep my ears open."

"I'll look for you at twelve-thirty, then." Mr. Drew pushed back his chair and glanced at his watch. "I must hurry now or I'll be late getting downtown."

After her father had left, Nancy Drew finished her breakfast and then went to the kitchen to consult with Hannah, the maid, concerning the work of the day. Although only sixteen, Nancy was unusually capable, and under her skillful direction everything ran smoothly in the Drew household.

On the death of her mother six year before, she had taken over the entire management of the establishment. The Drews employed one servant, Hannah Gruen, an elderly maid of all work who had been with them for many years.

The responsibility of the household might have weighed heavily upon Nancy, but she was the type of girl who is capable of accomplishing a great many things in a comparatively short length of time. She enjoyed sports of all kinds and she found time for clubs and parties.

In school Nancy had been very popular and she boasted many friends. People declared that she had a way of taking life very seriously without impressing one as being the least bit serious herself.

While at school Nancy had made one particular chum, Helen Corning, of whom we shall hear more later. She had also made two enemies, the Topham sisters. Once she had caught Ada in wrongdoing in class and both sisters had placed the blame on Nancy. But Helen and two others had come to Nancy's rescue. Since that time Ada and Isabel had been more hateful to Nancy than ever.

"I'll not be back for luncheon to-day," Nancy told Hannah, as she prepared to leave the house. "I have made out the dinner menu and ordered the groceries, so I guess you won't need me for a few hours."

Leaving the house, she went to the garage where she kept her automobile. It was a shining new blue roadster, the birthday gift of her father.

Quickly backing the automobile to the street, she set off for the shopping district. She drove swiftly down the boulevard, and upon reaching the more congested streets, wormed her way skillfully through heavy traffic.

Entering a department store, she made a number of small purchases on the main floor and then went directly to the wearing apparel section, as it was her intention to purchase a frock suitable for the afternoon party to which she had been invited.

Usually, Nancy found the service excellent, but this morning was an especially busy one and an extra rush of customers had temporarily overwhelmed the sales force.

She did not mind waiting her turn, but quietly sat down in a convenient chair and glanced about with interest. After a time her attention was attracted toward two girls who, like herself, were waiting for an available saleswoman, but less patiently. Instantly, Nancy recognized them as Ada and Isabel Topham.

They were remonstrating with the floor manager, and their voices carried so far that she could not help hearing what they said.

"We've been standing here nearly ten minutes!" Ada said petulantly. "Send a saleswoman to us immediately!"

"I am afraid I can't," the floor manager said regretfully. "There are a number of others ahead of you. An extra rush of customers——"

"Perhaps you don't know who we are!" Ada interrupted rudely.

"Indeed, I do," the floor manager told her, with a trace of weariness. "I will have a sales-

woman here in a few moments. If you will
only wait——"

"We're not accustomed to waiting," Isabel
Topham told him icily.

"Such service!" Ada chimed in. "Do you
realize that my father owns stock in this store?
If we report your conduct to him, he could
have you discharged."

"I'm sorry," the harassed floor manager
apologized. "But it is a rule of the store.
You must await your turn."

Ada tossed her head and her dark eyes flashed
angrily. In spite of the expensive clothes she
wore, she was anything but attractive, for she
was tall and slender to the point of being
termed "skinny." Now that her face was dis-
torted with anger, she was positively ugly.

Isabel, who was the pride of the Topham
family, was rather pretty in a vapid sort of
way, but Nancy Drew thought that her face
lacked character. She had acquired an arti-
ficial manner of speaking which was both irri-
tating and amusing. It was her mother's
ambition that some day she marry into a
wealthy family, and every opportunity was
given her for a brilliant match.

The two sisters were older than Nancy, but
had been in her class at school. She had found
them stupid, as well as arrogant. They had

never been popular with their classmates and had boasted few friends.

Now, as they turned from the floor manager and saw her for the first time, Nancy bowed.

Isabel coldly returned the bow but did not speak a word of greeting. Ada gave no indication that she had even noticed her.

"Snobs!" Nancy told herself. "The next time I won't even bother to speak to them!"

At that moment a saleswoman hurried toward the Topham girls and at once they began to shower abuse upon her for her failure to wait upon them sooner. Nancy watched them curiously as they examined the gowns which the saleswoman brought out for their approval. Evidently, Isabel and Ada were in an unpleasant frame of mind, for they tossed aside beautiful creations of lace and chiffon with scarcely a second glance. They found fault with everything.

"A very chic gown," the saleswoman told them hopefully, as she displayed an attractive dress. "It is a Paris model and arrived this morning."

Ada picked it up, gave it one careless glance, and then tossed it into a chair. The gown slipped to the floor in a crumpled mass, and, to the horror of the saleswoman, Ada stepped on it as she turned to examine another dress. In disgust, Nancy moved away and began to examine a rack of dresses in another part of the room.

Presently, as she wandered back, she saw that Ada and Isabel were leaving without having made a purchase. As they swept past, Ada brushed against her. Instead of apologizing, she wheeled and surveyed Nancy coldly.

"Do watch where you are going!" she said tartly.

Nancy stifled a sharp retort and made no reply. Not without amusement she watched the Topham sisters as they flounced to the elevator.

"I don't wonder that people say such mean things about them," Nancy told herself.

Her thoughts were cut short as a saleswoman offered her services. It was the same girl who had waited upon the Topham sisters.

Nancy quickly selected a party frock of blue crêpe which matched her eyes, and went to the fitting room to try it on.

"It's a real pleasure to serve you, Miss Drew," the saleswoman assured her when they were alone. "But how I dread to see the Topham sisters come into the store! They are so unreasonable."

"Ada and Isabel aren't very popular," Nancy agreed. "They seem to think their word is law."

The saleswoman sighed.

"And I'm afraid it will be if they get all of Josiah Crowley's money." She lowered her voice. "The estate hasn't been settled, but they're counting on the fortune already. I heard Miss Ada say to her sister: 'Oh, I guess we'll get all of old Crowley's fortune as soon as the lawyers stop squabbling.' But it's my opinion the Tophams are mightily worried for fear somebody will show up with a later will which may do them out of most of it."

Nancy was far too wise to engage in gossip with the saleswoman, for she could not tell how far anything she might say would be carried. But she was interested in the information. The fact that the Tophams were worried indicated to her that they were of the opinion that Josiah Crowley had made a second will. Evidently, they were somewhat disturbed by the claims of the other relatives.

Ordering the frock which she had purchased sent to her home, Nancy glanced at her watch and saw that it was after twelve o'clock.

"I must hurry or I'll be late in meeting father," she thought, and left the store.

She drove directly to her father's office, and although a few minutes ahead of the appointed time, found that he was ready to leave.

"What luck, father?" Nancy demanded eagerly, when they were alone in the inner office.

"Did Mr. Rolsted promise to take luncheon with you?"

"Yes. We are to meet him at the Royal Hotel in ten minutes. Do you still think I should quiz him about the Crowley will?"

"Oh, I'm more than ever interested in the case, father. I can't tell you why, but I just seem to know that Josiah Crowley made a second will."

"Well, your intuitions are frequently correct, Nancy," Mr. Drew smiled. "So I'll do my best to find out what Mr. Rolsted knows about the case. However, I must warn you not to appear too eager for information, or he may suspect we have a dark motive behind the luncheon invitation."

"I'll be careful," Nancy laughed.

The Royal Hotel was located less than a block away, and Nancy and her father quickly walked the distance. As they entered the lobby they found Mr. Rolsted there ahead of them. Carson Drew introduced his daughter, and the three made their way to the dining room where a table had been reserved for them.

At first the conversation centered about a variety of subjects. As the luncheon progressed the two lawyers began to talk enthusiastically of their college days together and finally of their profession. Nancy began to fear that the subject of the Crowley estate never would be brought up.

Then, over the coffee cups, Carson Drew skillfully swung the conversation into a new channel and began to discuss strange cases which had fallen into his hands.

"By the way, I haven't heard the details of the Crowley case. How are the Tophams making out? I understand the relatives are trying to break the will."

For a moment Mr. Rolsted remained silent, and Nancy began to think that he did not intend to enter into a discussion of the case.

"The case wasn't turned over to me, Carson," the lawyer said quietly. "But I confess I've followed it rather closely because of a special interest I happen to have in Crowley. As the present will stands, I do not believe it can be broken."

"Then the Tophams will get the entire estate," Mr. Drew commented.

"Yes, unless another will is uncovered."

"Another will?" Carson Drew inquired innocently. "Then you believe Crowley made a second one?"

Mr. Rolsted hesitated as though uncertain whether or not he should divulge additional information, and then with a quick glance about, lowered his voice.

"Of course, I wouldn't want this to get out," he began doubtfully.

"You may trust Nancy not to repeat," Mr. Drew observed, guessing what was in the lawyer's mind. "I've found that out by experience," and Carson Drew smiled upon his daughter.

"Then I will say this much—it would not surprise me if another will should come to light. The Tophams treated Crowley most unkindly after he had made his will in their favor. About a year ago Crowley came to my office and told me that he wanted to draw up a new will. He indicated that he intended to cut the Tophams off without a cent. He expressed a desire to write the will himself, and asked me a number of questions. I told him exactly how to proceed. When he left my office he promised that he would have me look over the document when he had drawn it up."

"Then you actually saw the will?" Mr. Drew asked in surprise.

"No, strange to say, Crowley never came back. I don't know whether he drew up the will or not."

"And if he did, there would be an excellent chance that it would not be legal I suppose."

"Yes, it's a real trick to draw up a will that cannot be broken. But Josiah Crowley was a very careful man."

"Still, if he left even a loophole, the Top-hams would drag the matter into court."

"Yes, it is a foregone conclusion that the Tophams will keep the fortune whether they have a right to it or not. They have the advantage of money, you know. I believe the other relatives have filed a claim, but they have no proof a second will exists, and without money they cannot hope to fight the Tophams."

While her father and Mr. Rolsted discussed the case, Nancy Drew remained silent, but not a word of what was said escaped her. Although she gave no indication of her feelings, the information excited her.

After a time, Mr. Drew paid the luncheon check and the three arose and left the dining room. Mr. Rolsted took leave of them in the lobby.

"Well, Nancy, did you find out what you wanted to know?" Carson Drew inquired after the lawyer had disappeared.

"Oh, father, it's just as I suspected! Mr. Crowley did make a second will!"

"You mustn't jump hastily at conclusions," Mr. Drew warned her. "It's possible that Crowley never drew up the will at all, or if he did, he may have destroyed it."

"That's possible, of course. But he had no love for the Tophams, and I have a feeling he hid the will someplace. Oh, if only I could find it!''

"It would be as easy as looking for a needle in a haystack,'' Mr. Drew replied. "If I were you, I would forget about the case, Nancy.''

"I can't forget about it until I've at least made an attempt to find out what became of that will,'' Nancy insisted stubbornly.

"All right, dig into the mystery if you like, but I'm afraid you've set yourself an impossible task. I don't see how you hope to discover what became of the will when you haven't even a clue.''

"I'll find a way!'' Nancy laughed. "Give me time and I'll surprise you!''

But after she had said good-bye to her father and was slowly driving toward home, doubt assailed her. She knew that the odds were against her. Although she was determined to find out what had become of the Crowley will, she was at a loss to know how to begin. As her father had reminded her, she did not have a single clue.

" 'Where there's a will, there's a way,' '' she quoted whimsically. "That old proverb is doubly true in the Crowley case. If there actually is a second will, I'm going to find it! And if I do, I hope it won't prove to be in the Tophams' favor!''

CHAPTER III

RACING THE STORM

"NANCY, if you haven't planned anything special for the day, I wonder if you would care to do a little errand for me?" inquired Carson Drew one morning at the breakfast table.

"Why, of course," Nancy agreed pleasantly. "What is it?"

"I have a number of legal documents which must be delivered to Judge Hartgrave at Masonville some time before noon. I would take them myself, but I have several important appointments this morning."

"I'll be glad to do the errand for you," Nancy promised willingly. "I can run over to Masonville in the roadster. It isn't more than a fifteen mile jaunt."

"Fine. That's a load off my mind. You're sure you don't mind?"

"It's such a wonderful day, I'll enjoy the trip."

Mr. Drew parted the curtains at the dining-room window and looked out.

"It is a bright day, but I can't say I like

the appearance of those clouds in the west, Nancy. I'm afraid it may rain. You know how quickly our storms come up.''

"I'll start just as soon as I can get ready then. Where are the papers?''

"At the office. We can ride down together.''

Nancy Drew hurried away to find her hat and purse. Before Mr. Drew had collected his own belongings, she had backed the roadster from the garage and was waiting for him at the curbing.

"I haven't heard you mention the Crowley case lately,'' Mr. Drew commented as they rode along together. "Have you forgotten about it?''

Nancy's face clouded.

"No, I haven't forgotten, but I must admit I have made no progress. I guess I'm not cut out for a detective!''

"Don't feel discouraged, Nancy. The Crowley case would baffle a professional.''

"I haven't given it up yet, father. I may stumble onto a clue one of these days.''

When they reached the law office, Nancy stopped the roadster and her father got out. He disappeared inside the building and, returning a few minutes later, placed a fat manilla envelope in Nancy's hand.

"Give this to Judge Hartgrave. You know where to find him?''

"Yes, I'll have no trouble in finding his office. I've frequently driven as far as Masonville."

Selecting the shortest route to her destination, Nancy deftly shifted gears and was off. As she rode along the gravel road her eyes traveled to the fields on either side of the highway. Like a true daughter of the Middle West, Nancy Drew took pride in the fertility of her State and saw beauty in a crop of waving green corn as well as in the rolling hills and the expanse of prairie land.

More than once Nancy glanced anxiously at the sky. The sun shone down on the gravel road with dazzling intensity, but a large black cloud had settled in the west. Still, it did not appear to be rolling up very fast, and Nancy told herself that there was no need to worry.

"It won't rain for an hour or two, and by that time I'll be home," she thought.

Nancy took her time on the road and it was nearly eleven o'clock when she finally drove into Masonville. She went at once to Judge Hartgrave's office but was informed that he had gone to the courthouse. Nancy knew that the legal papers which she had been sent to deliver were important, and rather than leave them with the office girl she set off in search of the judge.

She had considerable trouble in finding him,

and it was nearly twelve o'clock when at last she delivered the manilla envelope into his hands. Learning that Nancy was the daughter of Carson Drew, Judge Hartgrave insisted that she take luncheon at his home before returning to River Heights.

Nancy accepted the invitation and spent a very pleasant hour in company with the judge and his wife. When at last she had insisted that she must start for home, it was after one-thirty.

"I have half a notion to take a different route back," she told Judge Hartgrave, as she stepped into her blue roadster. "It's a beautiful drive on the River Road. But the trip will take longer, and I am afraid it may rain."

Judge Hartgrave looked up at the sky, but, in spite of a general murkiness, the sun was shining.

"Oh, I don't believe it will rain for an hour or two," he said optimistically. "That big cloud is only bluffing."

"Then I'll take the River Road," Nancy decided.

She said good-bye and started the motor. Soon she was spinning along the road which wound in and out along the Muskoka River. Nancy met few automobiles, for the road was infrequently traveled. She did not hurry, but took time to enjoy the scenery.

Overhanging trees with dense foliage shaded the road and formed a tunnel which all but blotted out the sky. Presently, as Nancy drove into a clearing, she was astonished to see how dark it had become.

Evidently, the big black cloud which had attracted her attention earlier in the day was no longer bluffing. It had grown rapidly in size and was spreading over the sky in an alarming fashion. As Nancy Drew watched, the sun vanished as though by magic.

"How foolish of me to take this road," she chided herself. "I'm going to be caught in the storm! There isn't a chance that I can make it!"

Although the River Road was perfectly safe in dry weather, Nancy knew that a little rain would make it dangerously slippery. Then, too, the road was little traveled, and in case of accident she could not depend upon passing motorists for aid. If her roadster slipped into a ditch, it would be necessary to walk miles for help.

Few persons lived along the River Road, for the land was not considered valuable. In the spring of the year, with the arrival of heavy rains, the Muskoka River sometimes overflowed its banks and spread over the farmland, destroying the newly planted crops. For this reason, the district was not a popular one and the land was held by poor folk.

"If only I can find a farmhouse where I can drive in until the storm passes!" Nancy thought desperately.

The sky was now entirely overcast and in among the trees it was as dark as night. Nancy could not see the road distinctly, and switched on the headlights of her roadster. A brisk breeze began to stir the trees, and the leaves seemed to whisper a fearful warning of the storm to come. A feeling of uneasiness took possession of Nancy Drew.

She stepped on the accelerator and the roadster fairly leaped forward as though it, too, understood the need for haste. Suddenly, a flash of forked lightning coursed across the sky and was followed by a loud clap of thunder.

"That was close!" Nancy murmured uncomfortably.

She bent low over the wheel and took the curves as fast as she dared. An unexpected gust of wind struck the road and blew dust in every direction. As the cold air struck her, Nancy realized that the storm was almost upon her. Already, she could see the rain sweeping down upon her from the far hills.

Frantically, Nancy glanced about for a possible shelter. On down the road a short distance, she caught sight of an old farmhouse and a dilapidated barn which stood near the highway.

"If only I can get there before the rain strikes me!" Nancy thought anxiously.

But the storm would hold off no longer. Large drops of rain began to splash against the windshield, slowly at first, then faster and faster. The sky had taken on a yellowish cast.

Then, unexpectedly, came a second flash of lightning, and simultaneously a deluge of rain.

Nancy turned on the windshield wiper, but the rain was blinding in its violence. It was impossible to see more than a few feet ahead of the automobile, and almost in an instant the road had dissolved into a sea of mud. Nancy had been caught in a number of storms, but never one like this. She feared that she would slip into a ditch before she could reach the shelter of the barn.

Then, at the side of the road, the barn loomed up, and in relief Nancy saw that the doors were wide open. Without an instant's hesitation, she headed straight for the building and drove in.

Safely inside, she turned off the motor and the lights, and with a sigh of relief sank back against the cushions.

"Well, you got in just in time," said a pleasant voice behind her.

Startled, Nancy Drew turned quickly and saw a girl of her own age regarding her with interest. Even as the stranger spoke, the storm broke in full violence. A cold blast of wind rattled the barn doors and sent a sheet of rain inside.

"I beg your pardon," Nancy apologized, as she climbed from the roadster. "It wasn't very polite of me to run in here the way I did."

"You're more than welcome to the shelter, I am sure," the stranger told her kindly. "I'm afraid we haven't much else to offer."

In the semidarkness, Nancy studied the girl curiously. She had been impressed with her cultured voice and manner, and now she noted that her clothing, while not expensive, was neat and well made. The girl did not appear to be the daughter of a farmer who would live on this poor land, yet she seemed to fit into her background.

"It looks to me as though we're in for a real storm," the girl said and smiled pleasantly. She glanced outside at the pelting rain. "I'm afraid you'll be forced to remain here for some time."

"So long as I'm not out in the rain I don't mind," Nancy replied quickly. "That is, if you don't object."

"Object?" The girl spoke impulsively. "Oh, you can't understand how eager we are for visitors. Grace and I seldom have a chance to talk with anyone our own age. Sometimes a whole week will go by, and we won't see anyone but the postman."

Nancy Drew had a natural talent for unearthing interesting stories, and now a sixth sense seemed to tell her that she had encountered something unusual. She was eager to learn more about the girl and her reason for leading such an isolated life.

"I must thank you for your hospitality," Nancy said, with a friendly smile. "After all, perhaps the storm has done us both a real favor in throwing us together."

At the moment, Nancy Drew little dreamed that the next few hours were to reveal the truth of her polite utterance.

CHAPTER IV

AN INTERESTING STORY

"THE storm is getting worse every minute," Nancy Drew's companion observed.

Nancy followed her to the barn door and looked out. The rain was now coming down in torrents, and as the girls stood in the doorway a sudden gust of cold wind blew a sheet of water into their faces.

"Oh, let's get back where it's dry," Nancy laughed. "This is terrible!"

"It's getting cold, too," her companion announced, with chattering teeth. "Why not come into the house with me? It's far more comfortable there. And unless I'm mistaken, this storm will continue for an hour or so."

"I don't like to trouble you——"

"Oh, it's no trouble at all. Grace will never forgive me if I don't bring you inside." She turned to Nancy with an apologetic smile. "I guess I forgot to introduce myself. "My name is Allie—Allie Horner."

"And I am Nancy Drew."

"Not the daughter of Carson Drew, the noted lawyer?"

"Yes," Nancy admitted, in surprise. "Do you know my father?"

"Oh, no. But I guess everyone has heard of him." Allie Horner began to take off the raincoat which she wore. "Here, take this. And I'll find you a pair of rubber boots."

"I don't want to take your raincoat," Nancy protested. "What will you wear?"

"Oh, I have an old coat hanging here on a nail. I'll use that. Anyway, the rain won't hurt my dress."

Under protest, Nancy donned the raincoat and put on a pair of rubber boots which were several sizes too large for her. She made such a grotesque picture that the two girls could not help but laugh. Then they closed the barn doors.

"Now!" Allie directed. "Let's make a dash for it!"

Hand in hand they splashed through the mud toward the farmhouse. As they ran, a vivid flash of lightning momentarily illuminated the sky and caused the girls to cringe. The rain pelted down steadily, and the atmosphere was much colder than it had been ten minutes before.

"If it gets any colder we'll have hail," Allie

chattered, as the two girls reached the shelter of the porch.

Dropping their muddy boots outside, Allie flung open the door, and they entered a warm kitchen.

As the door closed behind them, an older girl who was bending over the kitchen range turned toward them in surprise.

"Grace, I've brought you a visitor," Allie said quickly. "Miss Drew, I want you to meet my sister. She's the mainstay of our little family."

Grace Horner cordially acknowledged the introduction and greeted Nancy with a warm smile. She was tall and slender, as was her sister, with dark hair and thoughtful brown eyes. Nancy judged that she was at least four years older than Allie. Her face was rather serious, and it was evident that responsibility had fallen upon her shoulders at an early age.

Nancy was at once attracted to both Grace and Allie, and responded to their cordial welcome.

"It's nice of you to take me in this way," she told them.

"Mercy! It's a pleasure for us," Grace assured her. "We don't see a girl of our own age once in a month unless we go to Masonville, and our visits there aren't very frequent, Miss Drew."

"Oh, please call me by my first name," Nancy begged. "Everyone does."

The three girls were soon laughing and talking together as though they had always been friends. Nancy knew that she was going to like the Horner girls, and it was evident they were delighted with her.

Presently, Grace deftly removed a cake from the oven and set it on the table to cool.

"Let's go into the living room," she suggested. "My cake is done, so I don't need to watch it. I'll give you a piece before you go, Nancy."

"And Grace's cakes are the real thing," Allie declared. "I'm not much of a cook myself. I'd rather be outdoors."

"We don't wish you any bad luck, Nancy," Grace laughed as she led Nancy into the next room. "But Allie and I don't care how long it storms!"

"Neither do I, so long as I get home before dark," Nancy replied.

Although the living room was warm and comfortable, it was nearly bare of furniture. The floors had been painted and were scantily covered with handmade rag rugs. With the exception of an old fashioned divan, an inexpensive table, a few straight-back chairs, and an old wood stove which furnished heat, there was little in the room. However, dainty white curtains covered the windows, and Nancy realized that although the Horner girls were poor they had tried hard to make their home attractive.

"Surely, you two girls don't live here alone, do you?" Nancy inquired.

Allie nodded.

"Grace and I have been living here ever since father died. That was two years ago. Mother passed away just before that," the girl added with a slight catch in her voice.

"But how do you manage? It must be dreadfully hard for two girls to run a farm by themselves," said Nancy, in wonder.

"Our farm isn't very large now," Grace said quietly. "We have only a few acres."

"I know you wonder how we live, but are too polite to ask," Allie broke in. "Grace helps a dressmaker at Masonville whenever she can get work. She makes all our clothes, too. And I raise chickens."

"Chickens?" Nancy asked, in surprise. "Can you make much at that?"

"Well, it all depends. This year the market hasn't been so high as usual, and the price of eggs has dropped, too. But I enjoy the work, and I could make it pay if only I could afford to start a flock of white leghorns."

"Allie is a regular outdoor girl," Grace explained, with a smile. "We divide our work.

I attend to the house, but she would rather be outside.''

''We get along very nicely in the summer,'' Allie went on. ''We raise vegetables and have enough for our own use. But in the winter it's hard. I don't know how we'll manage this year.''

''We'll find a way, Allie,'' Grace told her, with a brave smile. ''We always have.''

She arose from her chair and turned to Nancy.

''I'm sure you're not interested in our misfortunes. It's true that we're poor, but we can still offer a guest a cup of tea. Excuse me while I make it.''

It was on the tip of Nancy's tongue to protest, but she checked the words just in time. She knew that Allie and Grace were proud and that to refuse their hospitality would hurt their feelings.

''I wish I could help them,'' Nancy thought. ''But if I offer to pay for the tea they will be offended. Perhaps later on I can engage Grace to make a dress for me.''

In a few minutes Grace returned to the living room bearing a tray which had been covered with a clean white napkin. She poured the tea and served the cake with as much poise as though she were gracing an elegant drawing room.

"I never tasted more delicious cake in all my life," Nancy said warmly.

The three girls chattered over the tea cups and watched the rain beat against the windows. Presently, as Nancy noticed an unusual picture on the wall, she commented on its beauty.

"Uncle Josiah gave it to us," Allie told her. "If he were only alive now, things would be different."

At the mention of the name, Nancy started. Could it be that Allie referred to Josiah Crowley? It was very unlikely, she decided, yet only the week before her father had told her that there were two girls living on the River Road who should have figured in the will. The relationship would be worth investigating, Nancy told herself.

"Then your uncle is dead?" she inquired sympathetically.

"Josiah Crowley wasn't really our uncle," Grace replied. "But we loved him as much as though he were a relative." Her voice broke and for a moment she could not go on. "He lived next door to us—that was when mother and father were alive. All of our misfortunes seemed to come at once."

"He was the dearest man you ever saw," Allie added, taking up the story. "Some people thought him queer, but you never minded his peculiar ways after you knew him. He was so good and kind to us. We were neighbors for years—until the Tophams induced him to live with them. After that, everything was changed.''

"But he never liked it with the Tophams," Grace declared. "They weren't kind to him, and he used to sneak off to visit us. Didn't he, Allie?"

"Yes, he often said that we seemed like his own children. He brought us so many nice gifts. We loved him for himself and not his money, but after our parents died he hinted that he intended to see to it that we never came to want. I remember the very last day we ever saw him alive, he told us that he intended to mention us in the will. 'I have planned a big surprise for you girls. You'll see it in my will.' Those were his very words."

"And then the Tophams got everything," Grace said somewhat bitterly. "It isn't that we were expecting any of the money, but it does seem unfair that the entire fortune should go to them. They never cared a snap of their fingers for Uncle Josiah, and I don't believe he intended to leave his money to them."

"Perhaps you were mentioned in the will they say can't be found," Nancy suggested.

Grace and Allie exchanged significant glances and gravely nodded.

"That's just what we think," Allie announced.

"Can't something be done about it? It seems only fair that you should have your inheritance."

"I'm afraid there's nothing we can do," Grace said doubtfully. "You see, although we are certain a will was made in our favor, we have no actual proof. We haven't enough money to fight the case."

"The Tophams ought to do something for you girls."

"The Tophams?" Allie laughed scornfully. "They wouldn't give us a cent."

For some time Allie and Grace Horner talked of Josiah Crowley and his queer ways. To Nancy it was evident that the girls had loved the old man a great deal.

Presently, as the rain ceased and the sun threatened to break through the clouds, Nancy arose to leave.

"Your story has interested me a great deal," she assured the Horner girls. "It's possible my father can do something to help you—he is a lawyer you know."

"Oh, we weren't asking for help!" Grace interposed quickly. "I don't know why we happened to tell you so much."

"I'm glad that you did, and if I can I want

to help you. If my father asks you to come to his office in River Heights will you do it?"

"Why, yes, I suppose so," Grace admitted slowly. "But we have told you about everything we know concerning the will."

"My father is a wonder at unearthing hidden facts," Nancy declared.

"It's kind of you to tell your father about our case," Allie broke in. "We'd be so grateful if something could be done. We don't want a cent that doesn't belong to us, but it does seem as though we should have received a small inheritance."

"Don't build up your hopes until after I've talked with my father," Nancy advised them as she turned toward the door. "If anything can be done I promise I'll let you know."

CHAPTER V

A CONFERENCE

ALTHOUGH the rain was no longer falling, the River Road was a sea of mud, and before Nancy Drew started for home, the Horner girls insisted on helping her put chains on the rear wheels of the roadster.

"You'll never make it to the gravel unless you do," Grace advised her. "The River Road is terribly slippery in wet weather. You're sure you want to attempt it? We'd love to have you stay with us until to-morrow."

"Oh, I'll have only two miles to go before I strike gravel," Nancy returned. "I'll make it all right. But before I go I do wish you would let me pay for all the trouble I have caused you."

"We couldn't think of accepting money," Grace said quietly.

"It's been fun having you here," Allie added.

At last, after thanking the Horner sisters for their hospitality, Nancy told them good-bye. Allie and Grace watched her until she had backed the roadster from the barn and was safely on the road.

"You're taking a big chance in this mud," called out Allie after her.

"If you have any trouble, come back here," added Grace. "That is, if you can get back."

"Don't skid into a tree."

"Or into a ditch—that would be worse."

"What are you trying to do, make me nervous?" demanded Nancy, but with a smile on her face.

"No; we only want to see you get home safely," answered Grace, and by that time the car was so far on its way no more could be said.

Once on her way Nancy had little trouble, for she was a skillful driver. The mud was heavy, but although the roadster slipped about she managed to keep it in the road. Nevertheless, she was relieved when at last she reached the main graveled highway.

"I'll stop at father's office," she decided, as she drove into River Heights. "I want to tell him about my adventure right away."

She parked the car and surveyed it rather ruefully as she climbed out.

"Poor thing needs a bath! But even if I did get into mud, it was worth it. Otherwise I would never have found out about the Horner girls."

As Nancy was admitted to her father's private office, he arose from his chair to greet her.

"I'm glad you're here safe and sound," he declared, in relief. "I've been worried ever since that storm came up. I telephoned the house and Hannah said you weren't back. It gave me a bad scare."

"I had a little adventure," Nancy announced, with an important air.

Quickly, she told of her meeting with the Horner sisters and what she had learned concerning the Crowley will.

"Allie and Grace Horner are as poor as church mice, but they're proud, too," Nancy ended. "If only we could do something to help them! They deserve a portion of the Crowley estate, but they'll never get it unless someone takes a hand."

"From what you say it looks as though Crowley really did make a will in their favor," Carson Drew commented thoughtfully. "I never had any particular liking for Richard Topham, and I'll admit it would please me to see him lose the money. I'll be glad to do anything I can to help the Horner girls, Nancy. We might invite them to the house for a little conference."

"I was hoping you would suggest that."

"You say the girls have no idea what became of the will?"

"They never saw it."

"Well, it's possible that by talking with them we may learn something which may serve as a clue."

"I'll invite them to the house to-morrow if you want me to," Nancy said quickly. "You're so clever at asking questions, and the Horner girls will do anything in their power to help."

Mr. Drew studied his desk calendar for a moment.

"All right. But make it day after to-morrow afternoon at three. I have no appointment for that hour."

Now that she had accomplished her purpose, Nancy gave her father a hug and fairly danced toward the door.

"I knew you'd try to help them," she called back over her shoulder. "Now that you've promised, I'll scamper off and let you get your work done!"

Nancy's interest in the Crowley case had intensified since her chance meeting with the Horner girls, and it was with impatience that she awaited the conference.

All the day of the appointment she kept watching the clock, wondering if Allie and Grace would keep the engagement. She had sent them the invitation and they had promised to come, but Nancy was a trifle uneasy, especially as the hour of three approached and the two girls had not arrived.

"I don't see why they don't come," she fretted.

The words were scarcely out of her mouth when the doorbell jangled.

"That must be the girls now," she cried, as she hurried to open the door.

It was indeed Allie and Grace Horner. Nancy greeted them enthusiastically and, ushering them into the comfortable study, introduced her father. At first the Horner sisters were rather ill at ease, but after a few minutes they relaxed and began to talk frankly.

"Tell me about Josiah Crowley," Carson Drew suggested. "I understand that he was rather a peculiar man."

"Oh, he was," Allie began impulsively. "I've seen him go about hunting for his spectacles when they were on his nose all the time."

"Did he ever hide things?" Mr. Drew inquired.

"Did he?" Allie laughed. "He was always putting things away in what he called a safe place. The place was usually so safe that he could never find it again!"

"Did he ever say anything which would lead you to believe that he had hidden a will?"

Allie shook her head.

"Not that I can remember."

"Why, he did, too!" Grace broke in. "One day when he was at our house he got to talking about the Tophams and the way they were trying to get his money. 'I guess they'll be fooled all right when they find out I've made another will,' he said with that odd little chuckle of his. 'This time I'm not going to trust it to any lawyer. I'll put it away in a place that I know will be safe.' ''

"That's right," Allie agreed. "I had forgotten."

"Was Crowley living with the Tophams at the time he told you this?" Carson Drew asked quickly.

Grace nodded.

"Do you think it possible that he hid the will somewhere in the house?"

"You mean at the Tophams?" Grace inquired. "Of course I have no way of knowing, but it's my opinion that he did."

Nancy and her father exchanged quick glances as the same thought occurred to them. Perhaps the Tophams had discovered the will and already had destroyed it!

Carson Drew asked a few more questions. The Horner girls were eager to help, but they were unable to furnish additional information which had a direct bearing on the missing will. After Nancy had served tea, they thanked Carson Drew for his interest in them, and arose to depart.

"If I find that I am able to help you in any

way, I will do so," Mr. Drew told the sisters
as he escorted them to the door. "And of
course there will be no charge for my services.
However, unless the will is found there is really
very little that can be done."

After Allie and Grace had left, Nancy turned
inquiring eyes upon her father.

"Charming girls," he commented, "and undoubtedly deserving."

"Then you'll help them?" Nancy demanded
eagerly.

"I am afraid there is nothing I can do,
Nancy," Mr. Drew returned regretfully. "The
will is probably lost forever. It wouldn't surprise me if it had been destroyed."

"You mean—the Tophams?"

Carson Drew nodded.

"The same thought came to me," Nancy declared. "It would be just like them to destroy
it if it fell into their hands! They have no
scruples whatsoever."

"Of course we have no proof the Tophams
did away with the will, Nancy. It would be
very unwise to suggest such a thing to the Horner girls. They deserve a portion of the estate,
but without the will nothing can be done. If
they took the matter to court they wouldn't
have a chance to win."

"I suppose you're right," Nancy admitted
unwillingly.

But while she dropped the subject for the time being, Nancy Drew did not forget the Horner sisters. She continued to hope that by some queer twist of fate they would come into their rightful inheritance.

"If the will has been destroyed I don't see how anyone can help them," she told herself rather unhappily. "But until I'm sure of it, I'm not going to give up!" She squared her shoulders with determination. "I'll find some way to discover what became of the will!"

CHAPTER VI

An Unpleasant Encounter

IN SPITE of Nancy Drew's firm decision to assist the Horner girls, the days slipped by and, try as she would, she could think of no way to discover whether or not the missing Crowley will had fallen into the hands of the Tophams. Although she seldom discussed the case with her father, he knew that she was troubled.

"You're worrying about the Horner girls," he observed one day. "I am afraid you are taking their misfortunes too seriously. There is nothing you can do without the will, and you had best forget about it. Why, you've scarcely been out of the house since the Horner girls were here. Go shopping, or anything, to take your mind from the subject."

"I have been thinking about Allie and Grace," Nancy admitted, with a rueful smile. "I was so sure I could do something for them."

"Give your mind a rest and perhaps you'll have an inspiration," Mr. Drew encouraged her kindly.

"All right, I'll take your advice and go shopping, though I really haven't a thing to buy. The fresh air will do me good, I suppose."

After luncheon, Nancy left the house and made her way toward the business section of River Heights. The walk was a long one, but she took it at a brisk pace. Nancy naturally was athletic, and as she swung along more than one passerby turned to look after her in admiration.

After "window shopping" for a time, she wandered into a department store more from curiosity than because she had anything to buy. She moved about aimlessly, gazing at whatever struck her fancy.

Suddenly Nancy's attention centered upon two girls who were hurrying down the aisle ahead of her. She stopped short and stared. Though their backs were turned, she had recognized them.

"Ada and Isabel Topham! I'm sure I don't want to tag them around! I'll just slip down another aisle!"

But Nancy Drew never carried the thought into action, for at that very moment she saw Ada brush carelessly against a counter of expensive vases. As her sleeve caught, a large fragile bowl was swept to the floor. In horror

Nancy heard the crash and saw the bowl break into a dozen pieces.

As Ada looked down upon the wreckage, a slight flush mounted to her cheeks. Then with a toss of her head, she started to move on.

"Miss, I am afraid I must ask you to pay for the bowl," a saleswoman interposed politely.

Ada wheeled angrily and stared at the saleswoman insolently.

"I'll not pay for it!" she snapped. "I didn't break it!"

"But, Miss, I saw you knock it off the counter," the saleswoman protested.

By this time the floor manager had arrived upon the scene, and a number of shoppers had gathered about Ada and the salesgirl. Nancy likewise drew closer.

"This impudent girl claims I broke a vase," Ada stormed, addressing the floor manager. "I wasn't even near the counter at the time! However, I did see her knock it to the floor herself. Isn't that so, Isabel?"

Solemnly, Isabel agreed to the untruth.

The floor manager looked doubtfully from the Topham sisters to the saleswoman. He realized that it would be a serious error to accuse well-to-do customers falsely, and for that reason he was inclined to give the Topham girls the benefit of the doubt. He stooped over and examined the fragments of the bowl.

"Someone must pay for the damage," he said severely. "This is an expensive imported bowl."

"Then let your clerk pay for it out of her salary," Ada retorted. "If she hadn't been so stupid she wouldn't have broken the vase!"

The saleswoman was too bewildered to take her own part and Nancy saw that the floor manager was in a dilemma. As she sensed that he was about to exonerate Ada from all blame, she stepped forward.

"You must be mistaken, Miss Topham," she said quietly. "I am certain the saleswoman did not break the bowl, for I saw the accident myself."

"What business have you to interfere?" Ada demanded harshly, wheeling upon Nancy.

"Perhaps it isn't my business, but I can't permit you to accuse this girl of something she didn't do."

"You saw the accident, Miss?" the floor manager questioned.

"Yes. As Miss Topham walked by the counter, her sleeve caught on the vase."

"It isn't true," Ada snapped. "But I'm tired of this silly argument. How much do you want for your vase?"

The floor manager studied a price list.

"Fifty dollars."

"What?" Ada fairly screamed. "You want fifty dollars for that old bowl? I'll never pay it!"

"The vase was imported from Italy, Miss, and I am afraid you must pay the price asked."

"Do you know who I am?" Ada inquired loftily.

"I think everyone in the city knows about the Richard Tophams," the floor manager returned wearily.

"My father owns——"

"He doesn't own this store," the man interrupted, with growing impatience. "If you refuse to pay for the vase I shall be forced to turn you over to the authorities."

"You wouldn't dare!" Ada gasped. "Never in all my life have I been insulted like this!"

Isabel, who was slightly more reasonable than her sister, now held a whispered conference with Ada.

"All right, I'll pay for the bowl," Ada decided, as she took out her checkbook. "But let me warn you the matter won't be dropped here."

She turned upon Nancy Drew and eyed her coldly.

"I'm not through with you either. young lady! You'll pay for this outrage!"

Nancy made no reply but continued to smile

pleasantly, an act which further enraged the Topham sisters. Hastily settling for the damage Ada had done, they sailed grandly out of of the store.

Gratefully, the saleswoman thanked Nancy.

"You don't know how I appreciated the way you took my part. I couldn't have paid for the bowl, and if you hadn't said what you did the floor manager probably would have discharged me."

"I saw her break the bowl and I was determined to see justice done. There is my name and address—if you need it," and Nancy handed the woman her card.

"I'm afraid you have made enemies by taking my part."

Nancy shrugged her shoulders indifferently.

"It really doesn't matter. The Topham girls were never my friends."

"But they may try to get even with you. They're very spiteful."

"Let them try!" Nancy smiled. "However, I don't believe there is any need to worry. Their talk is mostly bluff."

Lightly, Nancy Drew dismissed the subject, and, as she found she was being regarded with curiosity and admiration by those who had witnessed the scene, left the store. She walked slowly toward the park.

"It makes my blood fairly boil every time I

think of Ada and Isabel Topham getting all of the Crowley fortune," she told herself, with feeling. "Especially when Grace and Allie Horner need the money so badly. The way Ada tried to accuse that shopgirl was disgusting."

Nancy crossed the public park and paused for a moment at the drinking fountain. As she glanced up she saw that unwittingly she had selected the path Isabel and Ada Topham had taken. Upon leaving the department store they, too, had gone to the park and were now seated upon a bench engaged in earnest conversation. Their heads were close together, and, from the expression on their faces, Nancy suspected that they were discussing her. Unless she retraced her steps it would be necessary to pass directly in front of them.

"If they see me they are certain to say something mean," Nancy thought, "and if they do I'll be sure to lose my temper. I know!" she decided impulsively. "I'll take the path through the bushes and avoid them. I can pass behind that bench and they'll never notice me!"

Ada and Isabel were so engrossed in their conversation that they failed to notice Nancy's approach. Chuckling to herself, Nancy left the sidewalk and quietly made her way down the path which was shaded with overhanging bushes.

She had no intention of attempting to overhear what the Topham sisters were saying, but as she noiselessly approached the bench where they were sitting, two words reached her ears, causing her to pause involuntarily.

Ada was speaking, and the phrase which Nancy had accidently overheard was "the will." In a flash, her suspicions were aroused. She comprehended the significance of the phrase.

"It must be Josiah Crowley's will they're talking about," she reasoned. "Perhaps they know something about the missing will! They may reveal what became of it!"

With the instinct of a detective, Nancy Drew crept cautiously closer. The bushes were thick, and by crouching low behind the bench she was able to hear without being seen.

Oh, if only she might learn something which would prove that the Tophams had deprived the Horner girls of their inheritance!

CHAPTER VII

NANCY TURNS SLEUTH

WHILE Nancy Drew eagerly waited, scarcely daring to breathe naturally lest her presence be detected, Ada began to speak.

"Well, if there should happen to be another will, we may be dumped," she said sourly.

"I don't believe Josiah Crowley ever made such a will," Isabel replied, in so low a tone that Nancy scarcely caught the words.

"Evidently Nancy Drew does, or she wouldn't be taking such an interest in those Horner girls," Ada returned. "I know she had them at her house last week, because I was passing and saw them go in. How I hate that girl! If she should get her father interested, he might dig up another will."

"Even if another will does turn up, we can trust dad to take care of it," Isabel commented dryly.

"You mean he would——"

"Never mind what I mean," Isabel insinuated darkly. "Mother and dad wouldn't be simple enough to let that money get away from us. It's ours by right, anyhow. Didn't Josiah Crowley live on us?"

"Yes, we ought to have all of the money after enduring him for nearly three years. Just the same, I don't like the way Nancy Drew has taken up with the Horner girls. She always did have a way of nosing into things she had no business to find out!"

"Oh, pooh for her," Isabel scoffed. "Let her try to discover anything she likes. The money was given to us fairly enough."

The conversation ended abruptly as Isabel and Ada arose from the bench and walked on down the street. Nancy waited until they were out of sight and then emerged from the bushes.

"There may be a chance to find that missing will after all," she reasoned, as she sank down on the bench vacated by Isabel and Ada.

Nancy had always been convinced that Josiah Crowley had made a second will. However, since her talk with the Horner girls, she had shared her father's opinion that the document had fallen into the hands of the Tophams only to be destroyed. This conviction had discouraged her.

Now the information which she had gleaned from the snatch of overhead conversation, gave her new hope. From what Isabel and Ada had said, she was led to believe that if Josiah Crowley had made a second will, the Tophams were as ignorant as herself concerning its whereabouts.

"Anyway, it's encouraging to know the will hasn't been destroyed," Nancy told herself. "But there's one thing certain. If the Tophams ever get their hands on it, they'll take care it never comes to light. From what Isabel and Ada said I judge they're beginning to realize their position is anything but secure. If I'm ever to find that will, I must get busy before they beat me to it!"

Nancy Drew possessed her father's liking for a mystery, and she delighted in a battle of wits when championing a worthy cause. Carson Drew had often remarked that he enjoyed the detective work of his cases better than the court work, but Nancy knew he was too busy with his own cases to devote much attention to the missing Crowley will. If anything were done to help the Horner girls win their inheritance, she must accomplish it herself.

As Nancy reviewed the facts of the case, it seemed to her that she must have overlooked a possible clue. Never had a mystery appeared more baffling.

For nearly ten minutes Nancy sat lost in deep thought. Then, with a cry of delight she sprang to her feet.

"How stupid of me not to think of it before! The Horner girls aren't the only ones who should have figured in the will. There were a number of relatives, and father said that they filed a claim, too. I wonder who they are. If I could talk with them, it's possible I might learn something that would have a bearing on the case.''

Convinced that the inspiration was a happy one, she set off toward her father's office. He was engaged in an important conference when she arrived, and Nancy was forced to wait ten minutes before she was admitted to the inner office.

''Now what?'' her father asked, smiling as she burst in upon him. ''Is it a new dress you want?''

Nancy's cheeks were flushed and her eyes danced with excitement.

''Don't try to tease me,'' she protested. ''I've stumbled onto something important, and I want information!''

''At your service, Nancy,'' Mr. Drew said. ''But if it's about that Crowley case, I've told you everything I know.''

Nancy poured out the story of her encounter with the Topham sisters in the department store and told of the conversation she had overheard in the public park. Mr. Drew listened with interest until she had finished.

''And now what is it you want?'' he asked gravely.

"I thought if I went to those other relatives I might be able to learn something which may help solve the mystery."

"A good idea, Nancy."

"But I don't know their names, and that's why I came to you."

"I wish I could help you, but I'm afraid I can't," Mr. Drew said regretfully.

Nancy's face fell.

"Wait a minute!" he called, as she turned to leave. "I can't supply the names you want, but I think I can tell you where to find them."

"Where?"

"At the courthouse. They should be on file." He glanced at his watch and frowned. "But I'm afraid it is too late to go there this afternoon."

"Oh, and I'm anxious to find out right away," Nancy declared in disappointment. "If I delay even a single day the Tophams may get ahead of me and find that will."

Suddenly her face brightened as she thought of something.

"I know! I'll jump into the roadster and run out and have a talk with the Horner girls. They should be able to furnish me the information."

"You can try them, at least."

"That's just what I'll do," Nancy decided, as she turned again toward the door.

"Just a minute," Carson Drew stopped her. "I wonder if you realize just what you are getting into, Nancy?"

"Why, what do you mean?"

"Only this. Detective work isn't always the safest occupation in which to engage. I happen to know that Richard Topham is an unpleasant man when crossed. If you actually succeed in learning anything which may help the Horner girls, you are certain to have the Tophams in your wool."

"I'm not afraid of them, father."

"Good!" Mr. Drew exclaimed. "I was hoping you would say that. I'm glad you have the courage of your convictions, but I didn't want you to march off into battle without a knowledge of what, undoubtedly, you will be up against."

"Battle?"

"Yes, battle. Rest assured the Tophams won't give up the fortune without a bitter struggle. However, if they attempt to make serious trouble, I promise to deal with them myself. I only wish I had the time to help you find the will."

"And if I find it?"

"I'll take the matter into court."

"Oh, thank you! There's no one like you in all the world."

Nancy moved toward the door.

"I may not get back until rather late," she threw back over her shoulder. "I have a feeling I may discover a real clue to-day, and if I do, I'm going to trail it down!"

With characteristic impetuosity, she darted from the room, permitting the office door to bang behind her.

CHAPTER VIII

A Discouraging Day

AFTER leaving her father's office, Nancy Drew went directly home. Quickly backing her roadster from the garage, she set off down the River Road in the direction of the old farmhouse where the Horner girls lived.

Before leaving the main highway, Nancy glanced anxiously at the sky and was relieved that no clouds were visible.

"After my last experience, I don't intend to get caught in another storm," she admonished herself.

The recent rain had made the roads rough, and Nancy bumped about in the roadster rather uncomfortably. At last, however, she came within sight of the farmhouse, and as she viewed it from a distance noticed that it was even older and more run-down than she had thought.

The house was large and rambling, but apparently it had not been painted in years. Shingles were falling from the roof, and the porches sagged. As Nancy's eyes traveled to

66

the old barn, she wondered how it had managed to survive the recent storm.

"If Allie and Grace Horner only had money, they could make the place attractive," she thought as she drove through the open gate.

Squawking chickens fled before her as she stopped the roadster in the barnyard and switched off the engine. Springing lightly from the car, she ran up the walk toward the house. She paused at the kitchen door and rapped.

Receiving no response, she went around to the front of the house and knocked on another door. There was no answer. Nor did a tour of the yard reveal either of the Horner girls.

Disappointment took possession of Nancy. She had driven nearly fifteen miles only to find no one at home.

"I'm defeated at every turn," she thought disconsolately, as she slowly walked back to the roadster. "It's certainly discouraging."

"Hello, there!" a voice called. "Were you looking for us?"

The shouted greeting reached Nancy as she prepared to step into the roadster. One foot on the running board, she turned her head and saw the Horner girls hurrying toward her from the direction of the barn.

Allie did not wait for her sister to open the

barnyard gate, but, swinging easily over it, ran to meet Nancy.

"We saw you just as you were leaving the house," she cried enthusiastically. "We wouldn't have missed you for anything."

"We were picking berries in the woods," Grace explained, as she hurried up, slightly out of breath. Proudly she displayed a tin pail which was filled nearly to the brim with raspberries.

"But look at our arms!" and Allie laughed ruefully as she glanced down at the ugly scratches which had been caused by brambles and sharp thorns.

"You must come into the house and have a dish of berries, Nancy," Grace urged hospitably. "They're good with sugar and cream."

"If you don't have them too often," Allie added.

"I can stop but a minute," Nancy declared, as the three entered the house. "I came to talk about the will."

"Oh, then you have good news for us?" Allie asked hopefully. "Are we really going to get some of the money?"

"I don't know yet," Nancy was forced to admit. "So far I haven't been able to learn a thing about the missing will."

Allie's face fell, but she tried to hide her disappointment.

"We need the money so badly," she said, with an apologetic smile. "Grace hasn't had a new dress in three years. She makes all of our clothing out of old things we happen to have in the house. If our luck doesn't change soon I'm afraid we'll be mistaken for rag pickers."

"We really didn't expect much of Uncle Josiah's money," Grace broke in quickly, lest Nancy misinterpret her sister's remarks. "We weren't related, you know."

"Well, you can hardly say the Tophams were, for that matter," Allie declared. "They were third or fourth cousins."

"We can get along without the money," Grace said quietly. "We manage very well when I have plenty of work. We're a little discouraged right now because dressmaking has fallen off. It's a slack season. I guess people would rather go to the store and buy a dress readymade."

"I wouldn't," Nancy declared impulsively. "Grace, I'd like to engage you to make me a dress. Will you do it? I'll pay you well."

Tears of joy came into Grace's eyes.

"Will I? Oh, you don't know how grateful I am for the work. I haven't had anything to do for nearly three months. I don't mind poverty so much for myself, but for Allie—"

her voice broke. "I promised mother I'd look after her."

Allie sprang from her chair and rushed to her sister. She flung her arms affectionately about her.

"Oh, Grace, I shouldn't have said what I did about needing money. I didn't mean it! Truly, I didn't."

"But it's the truth."

"We'll get along, Grace. If only my chicken money came in faster! Why can't a hen lay more than one egg a day?"

Grace smiled faintly at Allie's feeble attempt at a joke, and, to break an awkward silence, Nancy took up the conversation.

"I'll bring the dress material with me the next time I come this way."

She did not need a new dress, but she realized that there was no other way to help the Horner girls, for they were too proud to accept money.

"And now I want to ask you a few more questions about Josiah Crowley," Nancy told them. "Do you know whether he ever visited other relatives besides the Tophams?"

"Oh, yes," Allie returned promptly. "He was only distantly related to the Tophams, you know. They were third cousins I believe. He had a number of other relatives whom he frequently visited."

"Before he went to live with the Tophams, they took turns keeping him," Grace informed her visitor.

"Can you tell me the names of these relatives?"

"Let me see," Grace lost herself in thought. "There are two cousins living in Masonville."

"Matilda and Edna Turner," Allie prompted her. "They're regular old maids, but awfully nice. They were wonderful to Uncle Josiah when he was alive."

"And there were two nephews," Grace went on. "William and Fred Mathews. They have a farm on this same River Road. Everyone thought they would get something."

"How far do they live from here?" Nancy inquired.

"Oh, not more than five miles. You could drive there in a few minutes. It's on the way to Masonville."

"Then I'll be able to make the two calls on the same trip," Nancy announced, as she arose to depart. "I must hurry along now or it will be too late for me to stop there this afternoon. I am hoping that by talking with the relatives I may learn something which will help us to trace the missing will."

"I'm afraid there's not much chance we'll ever get anything," Grace said rather morosely.

"The Tophams will never let the money slip out of their hands."

"If we find the will, they won't be able to keep the money," Nancy declared. "Father will see to it that you girls get your just due."

"Oh, Grace, we forgot to tell Nancy about Abigail Rowen," Allie reminded her sister. "She'd be apt to know more about the will than anyone else."

"That's right! You really should call on her, Nancy. She took care of Uncle Josiah one time when he was sick, and he thought the world of her. He often declared he intended to leave her something."

"Even a few hundred dollars would have meant so much to her," Allie added. "Abigail is old and feeble now. She must be more than seventy years of age, and there's no one to look after her."

"Where shall I find her?" Nancy asked quickly.

"She lives over on the West Lake Road," Grace responded. "It's a good many miles from here. You could make inquiry at some of the farmhouses along the road."

"I won't have time to go there to-day, but I'll surely call upon her as soon as I can. And now I must be going or it will be dark long before I get back to River Heights."

Nancy said good-bye hastily. The Horner

girls accompanied her to the roadster and watched her drive away. As she looked back from the corner, they waved their handkerchiefs.

"Plucky girls!" Nancy thought. "Until to-day I didn't realize how terribly they need help. I simply must find a way to help them!"

She drove along the River Road, heading in the direction of Masonville. Although it was growing late, Nancy was determined to visit the Mathews brothers, and, if possible, Matilda and Edna Turner.

After she had gone perhaps five miles, she began to watch the mailboxes, and presently noticed one which bore the name "Mathews." The farmhouse was set back a short distance from the road, and Nancy drove the roadster down a narrow lane which led to it.

As she stopped the car, a man came out of the house and regarded her questioningly. Learning that the farmer was William Mathews, Nancy quickly explained her mission. At first the man was inclined to distrust her, but after he had made certain that she was not a friend of the Richard Topham family, he talked frankly of Josiah Crowley and told all that he knew concerning the will.

"My brother and I have filed a complaint with the proper authorities at the courthouse," he explained. "We feel certain there must have been another will because Uncle Josiah always said that he intended to leave us something."

"Did you actually see the will?" Nancy questioned hopefully.

The farmer shook his head.

"No, my brother and I haven't the proof that he ever made a second will. But we do know that he never had any particular love for the Tophams. He felt that they took him in only because they were after his money, and I guess he wasn't wrong at that. Anyway, I am certain he had made up his mind to cut them off without a cent."

"Perhaps he neglected to write the second will."

"That wouldn't be like Uncle Josiah. He was rather queer about little things, but he was always particular in attending to business matters. No, I'm more apt to think he made the will and hid it somewhere."

"You have no idea where he could have concealed it?"

"Not the slightest, Miss. My brother and I will be glad to offer a substantial reward to anyone who can produce it."

Nancy asked a number of other questions, but the farmer was unable to furnish information which was of any value. Disappointed, she thanked the man for his trouble, and continued on her way to Masonville.

"Rumor! Rumor!" she sighed. "That's all I hear. At my next stop I hope I'll acquire a few facts!"

Upon reaching Masonville, Nancy made inquiry and was directed to the home of the Turner sisters. They lived alone at the outskirts of the city. Although not in poverty, they did not have any more money than they needed.

Nancy found them at home, and when they learned the purpose of her visit they greeted her cordially. They were very pleasant ladies and she spent nearly an hour at their home. But although they answered her questions willingly, she learned nothing which had a direct bearing on the missing will.

Matilda and Edna Turner insisted that Josiah Crowley had intended to disinherit the Tophams, but they had no idea what could have become of the later will. They had been led to expect a small inheritance, and were disappointed that everything was to go to the Tophams.

"Why don't you talk with Abigail Rowen?" Matilda suggested at the conclusion of the interview. "She took care of Josiah once when he was sick, and he thought a lot of her. She knew more about his queer ways than any other living person.''

''I don't believe it would do a particle of good,'' Edna interposed. ''Abigail is getting along in years, and her memory isn't what it used to be.''

It was after dark when at last Nancy took leave of the Turner sisters and headed her roadster toward home. She was tired and hungry as well as discouraged.

''So far I've only wasted my time,'' she thought despondently. ''I'm no closer to finding the will than I ever was, and I'm sure there is one. I've often heard father say that no real mystery is solved without a lot of hard work—and I'm ready to believe it!''

With the exception of Abigail Rowen, Nancy had called upon all of the Crowley relatives. From what the Turner sisters had told her, she was doubtful that a visit to her cottage would be worth while.

''Oh, well, I suppose I may as well go there to-morrow,'' Nancy decided, after a mental debate. ''She's my last hope. If I fail there, I'll be forced to give up.''

CHAPTER IX

Vital Information

"This must be the house. It certainly fits the description given me."

As she spoke Nancy Drew paused before a square, one-story frame building which stood dejectedly in the center of a yard overgrown with weeds and dandelions. The cottage was sadly in need of paint and pickets were missing from the sagging fence which enclosed it. A boardwalk which led to the front porch had begun to rot away, and offered treacherous footing.

"The place looks deserted, but I'm sure Abigail Rowen must live here," Nancy assured herself as she made her way up the walk, gingerly avoiding loose boards which threatened to fly up at her.

Early that morning she had left River Heights in her final quest for information concerning the Crowley will. Nancy did not know exactly where Abigail Rowen lived, but she had taken the West Lake Road and had made inquiry along the way. Neighbors had assured her that she could not miss the place, as it was the most run-down house along the road.

"If Abigail can't help me, I'm at the end of my string," Nancy thought, as she rapped on the front door.

There was no response to her knock and she rapped a second time. She was about to turn away in disappointment when a slight noise within the house attracted her attention. She was certain her rap had been heard.

"Who's there?" a muffled voice called. "If you're a peddler I don't want anything."

"I'm not a peddler," Nancy called out reassuringly. "Won't you let me in, please?"

There was a long silence, and then the quavering voice replied:

"I can't open the door. I've hurt myself and can't walk."

Nancy hesitated an instant, and then pushed open the door. As she stepped into the dreary living room, she saw the pitiful figure on the couch. Abigail Rowen lay huddled under a ragged old shawl, her withered face drawn with pain.

"I am Nancy Drew and I've come to help you, Miss Rowen."

At the words, the old lady turned her head and regarded Nancy with a stare which was almost childlike.

"You've come to help me?" she repeated

unbelievingly. "I didn't think anyone would ever trouble themselves about old Abigail again."

"Here, let me arrange the pillows for you." Gently, Nancy moved the old woman into a more comfortable position.

"Yesterday I fell down the cellar stairs," Abigail explained. "I hurt my hip and sprained my ankle. I can't take a step without it nearly killing me."

"Haven't you had a doctor?" Nancy asked in astonishment.

"There ain't been a soul come near me," Abigail sighed. "I've just laid here on my bed and wondered how soon the end would come. I'm getting along in years now and it won't be long——"

"Nonsense," Nancy protested brusquely, for she saw that the old lady's trouble had made her morose. "You have a good many happy years yet before you. Can you walk at all? Are you certain your hip isn't broken?"

"I can walk a little, but it hurts something awful when I do."

"Then your hip isn't broken," Nancy said, in relief. "Let me see your ankle. Why, you don't even have it wrapped up! Where are the bandages? I'll fix it for you."

"There's a white rag in the closet in the kitchen," Abigail told her.

Nancy shook her head sternly.

"A rag won't do. You have a bad sprain and it must be taken care of properly. You really should have a doctor."

' I can't afford it,'' Abigail murmured.

"Let me pay for it," Nancy begged.

Abigail shook her head stubbornly.

"I'll not take charity. I'd rather die in my bed."

"Well, if you're set on not having a doctor, I'm going to the nearest drug store and get bandages and a number of other things," Nancy insisted. "But before I go, I'll make you a cup of tea."

"There ain't any tea in the house."

"Then I'll get some. What else do you need?"

"I need 'most everything, but I can't afford to pay for it. You might get me some tea and a loaf of bread. That's enough. You'll find the money in a jar in the cupboard. It's not very much, but it's all I have."

"I'll be back in a few minutes," Nancy promised.

She stopped in the kitchen long enough to examine the cupboards. As she had suspected, they were practically empty. With the exception of a little flour and sugar and a cheap can of soup, there appeared to be nothing in the house to eat. Nancy discovered the money jar, but an investigation revealed that it contained less than five dollars.

"It's probably every cent poor Abigail has in the world," she thought.

Nancy did not take any money from the jar but quietly slipped out the back door. Hurrying to the roadster which she had left at the roadside, she drove to the nearest store and ordered nearly ten dollars worth of groceries. She wished that she might take a doctor back with her, but she realized that Abigail was set in her ways and would not accept the service since she could not pay for it.

Before she returned to the cottage, Nancy stopped at the drug store and purchased bandages and liniments. She carried the supplies into the house and quickly set about making Abigail more comfortable. She bathed the swollen ankle and bound it neatly with the clean bandage.

"It feels better already," Abigail told her gratefully. "I dunno what I'd of done if you hadn't come when you did."

As soon as she had attended to the woman's immediate needs, Nancy built a fire in the kitchen range and put on the teakettle. While she was waiting for the water to boil, she raised the drawn shades and permitted the warm sunshine to flood into the room. While she did this she told Abigail Rowen something about herself.

After the tea had steeped she poured Abigail a cup and urged her to eat the nourishing meal she had prepared. She was gratified to observe that almost immediately the old woman became more cheerful and seemed to gain strength. She sat up on the couch and appeared eager to talk with Nancy.

"There ain't many folks that are willing to help an old woman. If Josiah Crowley had lived things would have been different," she declared.

"It's strange that he didn't provide for you in his will," Nancy replied quietly.

She did not wish to excite the old woman by telling her real mission, and yet she was eager to find out what Abigail knew about the missing will. She hoped that she might lead her tactfully into a discussion of Josiah Crowley's affairs without raising hopes which might never be realized.

"It's my opinion that Josiah did provide for me," Miss Rowen returned impressively. "Many a time he said to me: 'Abigail, you'll never need to worry. When I'm gone you'll be well taken care of by my will.'"

"And then everything was left to the Tophams," Nancy encouraged her to proceed.

"That was according to the first will. But there was another one. I dunno what became of it."

"Are you sure there was another will?" Nancy inquired almost too eagerly, for Abigail looked at her rather sharply.

"Of course I am. I'm as sure of it as I am that I'm sitting here. Why, I saw that will with my own eyes!"

"You saw it!" Nancy gasped.

The old woman nodded gravely.

"Mind, I didn't see what was *in* the will. One day Josiah came in where I was sitting in my rocking chair, and right off I noticed he had a piece of paper in his hand. 'Abigail,' he said, 'I've made my will. I fooled them lawyers and wrote it myself.' "

"How long ago was that?" Nancy asked quickly.

"Let me see," Abigail frowned thoughtfully. "No, I can't remember the exact date. It was about the time Josiah went to live with Richard and Cora. Well, to go on with what I was saying—when Josiah showed me the will he seemed mighty tickled about it. Mind, he didn't show me what was inside but he hinted that he'd done well by me. 'But Josiah,' I said to him, 'are you sure it's legal to write it yourself?' 'Of course it is,' he said to me.

'A lawyer told me it was all right just so long as I had it witnessed.' "

"Do you know who witnessed the will?" Nancy broke in.

"No, I didn't ask him and he didn't say. He just went out of the room, chuckling in that funny way he had."

"Haven't you any idea what became of the will?" Nancy asked hopefully.

"I reckon he hid it somewhere. That would be like Josiah. But I remember he did say something about putting it 'where nobody can get it unless they have legal authority.' So I dunno what became of it. For all I know, he may have turned it over to a lawyer."

"Are you certain that was all he said?" Nancy inquired gently. She knew that Abigail had grown rather childish and that her memory was failing.

"It seems to me he did say something about what he was going to do with that will, but I can't just recollect." Abigail shook her head and sighed. "Many a night I've laid awake trying to think what it was."

It seemed to Nancy that as victory was almost within her grasp, it had been snatched from her. Undoubtedly, Abigail Rowen held the secret of the Crowley will locked in her brain. And it was equally likely that she would never be able to recall the vital information unless in some unusual way her memory was given a particular stimulus.

"Try to think!" Nancy begged.

"I can't remember," Abigail murmured hopelessly. "I've tried and tried." She leaned against the cushions and closed her eyes, as though the effort had exhausted her.

At that very moment the clock on the mantel chimed three. Abigail Rowen's eyes fluttered open and an odd expression passed over her face.

For an instant she stared straight before her and then slowly turned her head and fastened her eyes on the clock.

CHAPTER X

ABIGAIL'S DISCLOSURE

WHEN the mantel clock finished striking the hour of three, Abigail Rowen's lips began to move. Nancy Drew leaned forward eagerly, fearful lest a single word escape her. She sensed that the striking of the clock at a psychological moment had started a train of thought coursing through the old woman's mind, and now she believed that an important disclosure was about to be made.

"The clock," Abigail whispered so softly that the words were scarcely audible. "That was it! The clock!"

"Josiah Crowley hid the will in a clock?" Nancy prompted her.

"No," Abigail shook her head and sighed again. "That wasn't it. I thought I had it, and then it slipped my mind. I seem to recollect that he said something about a clock, but that wasn't it."

Abigail continued to stare at the timepiece, as did Nancy, who was at a loss to understand what connection it could have with the missing will. Suddenly, a low cry came from the old woman.

"There! It came to me just like that! After all these years——"

"Tell me," Nancy commanded quietly, for she feared that the knowledge might slip from the old lady before she could disclose it.

"A notebook!" Abigail brought out triumphantly. "It was something about a notebook!"

"Tell me more about the notebook," Nancy urged gently. Although she could scarcely hide her eagerness, she forced herself to speak quietly lest she excite Miss Rowen.

"I remember it all now. Josiah wrote about the will in a little notebook of his. One day he said to me: 'Abigail, after I'm dead if my will doesn't come to light, you can find out all about it in this little book of mine.'"

"What became of the notebook, Miss Rowen?"

"I can't seem to recollect. He hid it someplace."

Again Nancy Drew was baffled. Involuntarily, her eyes traveled to the mantel clock. She studied it critically. What connection could the clock have with the missing will, she asked herself. Certainly there must be one, for otherwise its striking would not have caused Abigail to think of the notebook.

Nancy had studied psychology in school and was familiar with the power of suggestion and association. Now her keen mind jumped to the conclusion that a clock had something to do with the missing Crowley will. Could it be that the notebook had been hidden in the clock?

Impulsively, Nancy got up and went over to the mantel. She took down the clock and looked inside. She saw nothing but a tiny key which evidently was used to wind the time-piece. Disappointed, she returned to her chair.

"Where was Josiah Crowley living at the time he told you about the notebook?" she asked the old lady.

"He was living in his own house then, but he was just getting ready to go to the Tophams. He'd been visiting around with his various kin and letting his own house stay empty. After the Tophams asked him to live with them, he sold his home."

"What became of the household goods?" Nancy inquired.

"Oh, the Tophams got 'most everything."

"There must have been a family clock," Nancy mused, half to herself.

"A family clock?" Abigail repeated. "Oh, yes, there was a clock."

"Can you describe it?" Nancy questioned.

"Well, it was just an ordinary mantel clock,

tall, and with a square face. Something like that one over there." The old lady pointed to the timepiece Nancy had just examined. "Only Josiah's was more elaborate. It had a moon or something on top."

"What became of the clock?"

"I dunno," Abigail responded indifferently. "I suppose the Tophams got it. They took everything else."

It was on the tip of Nancy's tongue to tell Abigail that Josiah Crowley might have hidden his will inside the family clock, but she hesitated to excite the old lady. After all, it was only a theory, and it would not be kind to encourage Abigail Rowen to believe there was a likelihood of gaining an inheritance unless it were a fact.

"I'll wait until I'm sure before I say anything about it to her," Nancy decided.

She asked a number of other questions, but it was soon apparent that Abigail had told all that she could recall about the will. Although Nancy spoke of the family clock a number of times, its mention did not seem to interest the old lady.

At last Nancy arose to depart, but before leaving she promised Abigail she would return in a few days to see how she was getting along. It was likewise her intention to stop at the nearest house to ask a neighbor woman to look after the old lady during her absence, but she said nothing of this, as she knew Abigail would protest.

After attending to the mission, she sprang into her roadster and started for River Heights.

Nancy Drew was highly elated at the information she had gleaned, and was now more interested in the case than ever.

"I'll not tell the Horner girls what I have learned," Nancy advised herself. "At least not until I have learned more about the family clock. If nothing comes of my theory, Allie and Grace would only be disappointed. I'll not raise their hopes until I have something important to tell."

As Nancy drove along on the West Lake Road she reviewed the facts of the Crowley case. Unquestionably, Josiah Crowley had made a second will. According to Abigail Rowen he had secreted it in a safe place and had written its location in a little notebook. He had told Abigail where the notebook could be found in case of his death, and with the passing years, the knowledge had slipped away from the old lady.

"It's my opinion that Josiah Crowley hid the notebook in the family clock," Nancy reasoned. "Otherwise, why would Abigail have said anything about it?"

Nancy was at a loss to know how to proceed. She knew that her next step in unraveling the mystery was to search the Crowley clock, but this would not be easy to accomplish. If, as Abigail had indicated, the clock had fallen into the hands of the Tophams, the task might be an impossible one. Then, too, it was not at all unlikely that the Tophams had already discovered the notebook.

"In that case they would have destroyed it," Nancy told herself. "Still, from the conversation I overheard in the park, I feel reasonably certain the notebook has never been found. No, if Josiah Crowley ever hid it in the clock, it must still be there, and it's up to me to get hold of it!"

During the long ride to River Heights, Nancy Drew mulled over the perplexing problem, but try as she would she could think of no way to get her hands on the old clock. She must find some means of gaining entrance to the Topham residence!

"I can't very well climb through a window, much as I would like to," she laughed. "And if I pay a social call upon the Tophams, they're sure to be suspicious. We haven't been friendly for years, and since Ada and Isabel discovered that I have taken an interest in the Horner girls, they would be certain to question my motive in going to their house. No, I must think of a good excuse!"

Presently, Nancy reached River Heights. She drove the roadster down the boulevard and stopped in front of her home. As she stepped out and was preparing to go into the house, she heard her name called. Wheeling about, she saw a girl running toward her. It was one of Nancy's chums, Helen Corning.

"Hello, Nancy," Helen called. "I haven't seen you for days. Where do you keep yourself?"

Nancy laughed as she greeted her chum.

"Oh, I've been especially busy lately. Come into the house and we'll have a chat."

"Oh, I can't, Nancy. I wouldn't be up this way, but I'm trying to sell tickets for a charity dance."

"How many have you sold?"

"I have six left." Helen sighed. "It's a thankless job."

"I'll take two if that will help you out," Nancy offered.

"Will it help me? Say, if I ever get rid of these tickets I'm going to dance a hornpipe. If I don't sell them this afternoon it's going to fix it so I can't start for Moon Lake. I wish I'd never promised to sell the things!"

"Moon Lake?" Nancy asked, in surprise.

"Yes, I'm going to a girls' camp there. I had planned to leave to-night; but unless I get rid of these tickets I don't see how I can. I wish you were going with me to Moon Lake, Nancy.''

"So do I, Helen.''

"Why don't you come along then?''

"Oh, I can't,'' Nancy protested. "I'm involved in something important and I can't get away. I'd love to go though—really, I would.''

"Well, if you find you can make it later, just hop into your roadster and come along. I'll be there for two weeks. That is, if I ever get rid of these charity tickets. I can't leave until I've sold them. I'd pay for them out of my allowance, only I've spent it already.''

"You are in difficulties,'' Nancy laughed. She reached in her purse. "How much are the tickets, Helen?''

"Two dollars each. How many will you take?''

"Oh, give me two.''

As Helen extended the tickets, a sudden thought struck Nancy Drew. A pleased light broke over her face.

"I have an idea, Helen! I'll sell all of your tickets for you! How will that suit you?''

"You're not joking?''

"Never was more serious in my life.''

"Then the tickets are yours. But let me warn you it won't be easy to sell them.''

"I'll enjoy trying it.''

"Well, I must say you have queer ideas of

fun," Helen commented dryly. "But I'll not argue with you. This will be fine for me. Now I'll be able to start for camp this afternoon. Here are the tickets." She handed them over with evident pleasure. "Good luck to you, Nancy. You'll need it!"

After Helen Corning had gone on down the street, Nancy Drew walked slowly toward the house. She regarded the charity tickets meditatively and chuckled softly to herself.

"That's once when I killed two birds with one stone! These tickets will serve as my passport to the impregnable Topham fortress!"

CHAPTER XI

Visiting the Tophams

It was nearly three o'clock of the following afternoon when Nancy Drew paused in front of the Topham residence on Highland Boulevard. She surveyed the structure with distaste.

The house was a large, pretentious affair of nondescript type. It was set back from the street and seemed to look down rather aloofly upon the surrounding homes. Even a casual glance at the lawn revealed that it had been "landscaped" with a vengeance. In an effort to "do it in proper style," Mrs. Topham had crowded the yard with sundials, benches, bird houses, and statues.

"Such lack of taste!" Nancy thought, as she walked up the path to the house.

She lifted the knocker on the front door. Nancy Drew realized that the interview was apt to be an unpleasant one, and she braced herself for the ordeal.

"I must be diplomatic," she advised herself, "or I'll not learn a thing about that clock.

If they suspect what I am about, they may bounce me out on my ear!"

At that moment a uniformed butler opened the door and condescendingly waited for Nancy to state her mission.

"Tell Mrs. Topham that Miss Drew is calling," she directed. "I am selling tickets for the charity dance. It's one of the most important social functions of the year. I am sure Mrs. Topham will wish to attend."

Nancy was forced to wait until the butler returned with permission for her to enter. As she was finally ushered into the living room, she could not help but smile at the elaborate formality, for in spite of Mrs. Topham's lofty ambitions, the woman had never achieved the commanding position in society that she strove for.

The room in which Nancy found herself was even more bizarre than she had anticipated. Expensive oriental rugs clashed with window draperies of a different hue. The walls were heavy with paintings which were entirely out of place in such a small room, and period furniture had been added indiscriminately.

But Nancy Drew was not interested in Mrs. Topham's lack of taste. As soon as the butler had left her alone she hastily glanced about. Almost at once her eye fastened upon a mantel clock which rested above the fireplace.

"I wonder if that can be the Crowley clock?" Nancy thought.

She rather doubted it, for the clock was too modern in appearance. She would have crossed the room to examine it, but a sound in the hall caused her to hesitate. As she heard someone coming she sank down on an uncomfortable ladder-back chair and assumed an expression of composure.

Mrs. Topham sailed grandly into the room and after surveying her for a minute, took a seat opposite Nancy.

"Well?" she demanded coldly. "What is it?"

"I am selling tickets for the——"

"I don't want them!" Mrs. Topham broke in rudely. "I can't be handing out my money to every peddler that comes along."

"Mrs. Topham, I am not a peddler," Nancy said cuttingly, as the color mounted to her cheeks. With difficulty she kept her temper in check. "Perhaps you didn't understand my name. I am Nancy Drew."

"Oh." A slight change came over Mrs. Topham's face, for she was fully aware that Carson Drew and his daughter were cordially welcomed in River Heights homes which merely tolerated the Tophams or, in a few cases, barred them. "I didn't catch the name, Miss Drew. What is it you are selling?"

"Tickets for the charity dance."

"Well, I hardly know what to say," Mrs. Topham hedged.

It was apparent that she was afraid to offend Nancy, and yet she was unwilling to part with the money. Although the Tophams were well-to-do, it was common knowledge that Mrs. Topham was decidedly stingy where other persons were concerned.

"How much are the tickets?"

"Two dollars each."

"Why, that's positively exorbitant!" Mrs. Topham protested.

"But we are selling the tickets for charity," Nancy explained. "I assure you the cause is an excellent one."

Before Mrs. Topham could reply, the front door opened and Isabel and Ada entered the house. Unaware of the visitor, they paused in the hall and carried on a disgruntled conversation. Evidently, they had been making social calls and were angry because some woman had refused to see them.

"Her maid said she wasn't at home, but I know she was," Nancy heard Ada complain.

The two sisters entered the living room, and when they saw Nancy stopped short and stared rudely at her. They did not speak a word of greeting.

"Miss Drew is selling tickets to a dance," Mrs. Topham informed her daughters.

"Don't buy them," Ada advised harshly. She had not forgotten the scene in the department store and longed to avenge herself upon Nancy, whom she considered responsible for her humiliation.

"But, Ada," Mrs. Topham protested feebly, "I thought it might help our social standing to take a few tickets."

"Don't be silly, mother," Ada snapped. "You'll only waste your money. We don't want to go, anyway."

"All right, I won't buy the tickets. Good afternoon, Miss Drew."

Reluctantly, Nancy arose. She was somewhat taken aback at the unceremonious dismissal, for she had not accomplished the real purpose of her visit.

As she turned, Nancy saw that Richard Topham blocked the door. He had entered so quietly that his arrival had been unobserved.

"Just a minute, Miss Drew," he said. "How many tickets have you there?"

"Four," Nancy gasped in surprise.

"I'll take them all."

With a grand gesture, Richard Topham opened his pocketbook and carelessly pulled out a twenty dollar bill.

"Keep the change," he ordered with assumed indifference. "Give it to the charity."

"Richard!" his wife gazed at him with disapproval. "Have you lost your mind? A twenty dollar bill!" she whispered.

"It's you who can't see beyond your nose," Mr. Topham retorted, but in a low voice. "You're always trying to get into society, and then you pass up a real opportunity. This donation will get our names into the paper."

He slumped into the nearest chair, and, opening the afternoon paper, buried himself in the stock page. Mrs. Topham knew that the matter was closed, for she scarcely dared speak to her husband when he was absorbed in the market reports. Nancy, too, realized that she had no excuse for prolonging her stay.

"I really must be going," she said quickly. "What time is it, anyway?"

"There's a clock in front of you," Isabel told her pointedly.

"Why, so there is," Nancy returned pleasantly. She glanced at the timepiece as though she had never seen it before. "Oh, surely that can't be the old Crowley clock? I'm so interested in heirlooms."

"I should say not! This is a far more expensive clock than the one Josiah Crowley left us," Mrs. Topham informed her caller condescendingly.

"Indeed? But I suppose you still have the family clock stored away in your attic. It's so hard to part with heirlooms." Cleverly, Nancy led Mrs. Topham to further disclosures.

"It wasn't hard to part with that old-fashioned thing," Mrs. Topham returned.

"We didn't want it cluttering up the attic," Isabel added. "Crowley left so much old junk."

"We considered the clock entirely out of place in our modern home," Mrs. Topham continued; "so we sent it up to our bungalow on Moon Lake."

Unwittingly, Mrs. Topham had given Nancy the information which she sought. The purpose of her visit accomplished, the girl politely thanked the Tophams for the purchase of the charity tickets and quickly took her leave.

As she walked down the path to the street she chuckled softly to herself.

"The Tophams may be old schemers, but this time they weren't so clever! Unless I am mistaken those tickets will prove the most expensive ones they ever bought! Before they get through it may cost them the Crowley fortune!"

CHAPTER XII

FOLLOWING A CLUE

ALTHOUGH highly elated at what she had learned from the Tophams, Nancy Drew was at a loss to know how to proceed. Undoubtedly, the old Crowley clock was set up in the bungalow at Moon Lake, but to get there was another matter. Nancy was determined to profit by the information, but was confronted with a number of serious problems.

Moon Lake was located among the hills forty miles away, and the roads were not of the best. Nancy did not know the exact location of the Topham cottage. Then, too, she needed an excuse for making the long trip.

"If the Tophams learn I have gone to Moon Lake they may become suspicious," she counseled herself. "I must think of some excuse to broadcast as a smoke screen."

But try as she would, Nancy could think of nothing. She took a certain amount of pride in her detective work, and now that she felt she had struck a valuable clue, she did not wish to ask advice from her father. She preferred to solve the mystery herself and then surprise him with the solution.

At dinner that night, Nancy was unusually silent and Carson Drew commented on her preoccupation.

"It seems to me you have been looking troubled lately," he observed. "Do you feel well?"

"Never felt better in my life," Nancy laughed.

"Just the same, I believe you need a vacation. I realize that it isn't easy for a girl your age to look after a big house like this. After a time, the responsibility gets to be wearing."

"How stupid of me!" Nancy exclaimed.

In her excitement, she permitted a fork to fall from her hand and clatter against the plate. Carson Drew, who did not comprehend what was passing through his daughter's mind, looked at her in surprise.

"Stupid?" he inquired.

"Oh, I mean it was strange I didn't think of Helen Corning before this," Nancy said hastily. "Helen is going to a girls' camp on Moon Lake. I'm dying to go to Moon Lake! May I start the first thing in the morning? I know I can get in. They have room for half a dozen more girls, Helen said."

"I think it would be an excellent idea, Nancy. A nice rest will do wonders for you. Go, by all means."

Nancy Drew was delighted that she had stumbled upon an excuse which would make it appear natural for her to go to Moon Lake. Early the next morning, after packing a suitcase, she started off in the roadster. As it was not out of her way to go by the River Road, she decided to stop at the Horners and give Grace the dress goods she had promised her.

As she drove in at the gate, one glance told Nancy that something was wrong. She saw a number of dead chickens in the barnyard, and as the Horner girls came toward her from the direction of the hen house, it was evident that Allie had been crying.

"Why, what is the matter?" Nancy asked quickly.

"Oh, it's my chickens, Nancy. They're all dying. I can't understand it. This morning when I went to feed them I found ten dead. I'm so discouraged."

"And yesterday a fox took two," Grace added. "I guess fate is against us."

"I'm afraid I'll lose all of my chickens before I get through," Allie declared unhappily. "I don't know what is killing them. They seem to have a strange disease."

"Allie is all broken up," Grace said quietly. "She's worked so hard with her chickens. Most of them are pets. And then, we need the money so badly. Now that dressmaking has fallen off, the chicken money is our only means of support.''

"Please, won't you let me help?" Nancy begged reaching for her pocketbook. "Accept a little loan to tide you over?"

Grace shook her head firmly.

"Thank you for your kindness, Nancy; but we can't take your money. We'll manage somehow.''

"If only Uncle Josiah had provided for us!" Allie sighed. "You haven't learned anything more about the second will, Nancy?"

"I haven't anything definite to report," Nancy replied, evading the question. She did not wish to raise false hope and she thought it best not to tell of her discovery. "But I'm still hoping we'll be able to trace the will.''

"I doubt it," Grace commented pessimistically.

"I'm on my way to Moon Lake now," Nancy told the girls. "I stopped here to deliver the dress goods." She handed a package to Grace. "The pattern is inside and I'm easy to fit, so you'll have no trouble.''

Grace's face brightened as she accepted the bundle.

"Oh, Nancy, I can't thank you——"

"It is I who should thank you," Nancy laughed. "And now let me pay for the dress in advance.''

Again Grace stubbornly shook her head.

"Not until the work is finished. That isn't good business."

Nancy saw that Grace and Allie were too proud to accept help, and regretfully abandoned the idea of trying to give them money.

"I'll come back in a few days for a fitting," she promised, as she prepared to drive away.

Nancy's talk with the Horner girls had left her rather depressed, for she realized that in spite of their pride, Allie and Grace would soon be forced to accept charity. Oh, if only she could help them!

"And poor old Abigail," Nancy thought. "If Josiah Crowley had used a grain of sense, things wouldn't be in such a muddle."

Nancy soon branched off from the River Road and headed south toward Moon Lake. The highway was little traveled and it was necessary for her to devote all of her attention to driving. The road had not been dragged after a recent rain and the ruts were deep. Jagged rocks and stones were scattered in the path, and it seemed to Nancy that the hills went straight up and straight down.

Presently, she noticed that the roadster had taken a strange notion to turn to the left of the road in spite of her efforts to keep it in the middle. Not without foreboding of trouble,

she stopped the car and got out to make a tour
of inspection. As she had suspected, a rear
tire was flat.

"A puncture!" Nancy murmured in disgust.
"If that isn't just my luck! Oh, well, I suppose I must fix it myself, because there won't
be another car along for an hour on this road."

It was not the first time Nancy Drew had
changed a tire, but she never relished the task.
Rummaging under the seat, she pulled out the
tools and quickly jacked up the rear axle. She
loosened the lugs which held the tire in
place, and tugged at it. Again and again she
pulled, but the huge balloon tire could not be
budged. Then, as she gave one mighty tug,
it came off and Nancy Drew fell backwards into
a sitting posture in the road.

"Well, it's off, anyway," she told herself
with satisfaction, as she brushed the dirt from
her clothing.

It required but a few minutes to put on the
spare tire and fasten the old one to the rear of
the car. Then, in relief, Nancy started on her
way again, but the accident had delayed her
nearly an hour.

It was after twelve o'clock when at last she
came within sight of Camp Avondale, where
Helen Corning was staying. Through the tall
trees she caught a glimpse of a long row of

shacks and saw the smoke rising from the cook house. Beyond, the blue lake sparkled and glimmered in the sunlight.

As Nancy drove into the camp, a group of girls gathered about the roadster. Helen Corning came running out of a cabin to greet her chum.

"Girls, it's Nancy Drew!" she exclaimed enthusiastically. "Now the fun will start! Park your car over there back of the cook house, Nancy."

"Am I too late for dinner?" Nancy demanded. "I'm nearly starved."

"You're just in time," Helen assured her. "Oh, Nancy, I'm so glad you came."

"So am I."

"How long can you stay?"

"Oh, I don't know. Until you get tired of me probably."

"Then you'll stay for the rest of the summer," Helen laughed.

Nancy was escorted to the main building of the camp, where she met the lady in charge and registered.

"She is to stay with me," said Helen; and so it was arranged.

When the girls walked off Nancy told Helen about selling the charity dance tickets and gave her the money paid by Mr. Topham.

"He surely was generous," said Helen, in surprise.

"He did it just to show off," declared Nancy. "I am positive of it."

Nancy scarcely had time to deposit her suit-case under her cot and freshen up a bit from her long ride, when dinner was called. The food was plain but substantial, and already she discovered that she had developed an enormous appetite.

Dinner over, she was rushed from one thing to another. The girls insisted that Nancy join them in a hike. She returned to camp with a desire for a good rest, but Helen Corning had other plans.

"We're all going for a ride in the launch before supper," she declared.

"Don't you ever rest here?" Nancy groaned.

"Oh, yes—at night. This is your first day here. You'll be used to it in a day or so."

"Either that or I'll be a wreck."

"But you don't want to miss the launch ride, Nancy. You'll have a splendid opportunity to see all the summer cottages on Moon Lake."

"Summer cottages?" Nancy asked quickly. Instantly she thought of the Topham bungalow and wondered where it was located. Undoubtedly, the launch ride would give her the opportunity to find out.

"You'll go, won't you?" Helen begged. "You can rest after supper."

"Yes, I'll go," Nancy promised. "You couldn't keep me here."

Although she was tired, she was really enjoying herself immensely.

Six girls loaded themselves into the launch and someone started the motor.

"It's always a relief when the engine starts," Helen explained. "Every so often it balks."

As the little launch turned out into the lake, it seemed to Nancy that she had never seen a more beautiful sight. The sun, which appeared to be sinking down into the water, resembled a great ball of fire. Yet, she did not forget the real purpose of the trip.

"The Tophams have a bungalow up here, haven't they?" she questioned.

"Yes, it's across the lake from here. We'll come to it presently."

"The Tophams aren't there now?"

"Oh, no, the cottage is closed. There's a negro caretaker who looks after it—they call him Jeff Tucker."

"Is it hard to get to the place?"

"Oh, not if you go by launch. But it's a long way if you take the road around the lake. I didn't know you were particularly interested in the Tophams, Nancy."

"Oh, they're no friends of mine," Nancy

returned hastily. "I was merely curious."

After a time, as the launch chugged along close to the shore, Helen waved her hand toward a bungalow which was set back some distance from the water.

"The Tophams own that one," she informed her chum.

Eagerly, Nancy turned her head and looked. She told herself that she would remember the location.

"We're going to have a wonderful time here together," Helen chatted happily on. "Next week there's going to be a big dance, too. Oh, there's so much of interest at Moon Lake, Nancy! You'll stay, won't you?"

Involuntarily, Nancy's eyes swept the shore and came to rest on the Topham bungalow.

"You're right, Helen," she agreed heartily. "There are a number of interesting things here! Yes, if you want me to, I'll stay."

CHAPTER XIII

An Adventure

Nancy Drew had made up her mind to visit the Topham cottage the very next day, but in making her plans she had counted without Helen Corning and her friends. They were unwilling that she should be alone even for a minute.

From the moment she awoke in the morning and sniffed the fragrant odor of the pines, she was rushed from one thing to another. After a breakfast of fruit, fried eggs, crisp bacon, and hot corn bread, she was pressed into a tennis game. The afternoon was devoted to swimming and water polo. By evening Nancy Drew was so tired she could scarcely keep her eyes open, and she was thankful for the opportunity of tumbling into bed.

"To-morrow I simply must find a way to visit the Topham cottage," she told herself just before she dropped off to sleep.

Immediately after breakfast the following morning, Helen Corning announced the plan for the day.

"The girls have decided on an all-day hike into the woods, Nancy. You'll go, won't you?" Nancy groaned.

"You're wearing me to a frazzle, Helen. Please let me off this time. I'd like to stay in camp to-day and just rest up."

"Well, all right," Helen agreed unwillingly. "I'll stay with you."

"Oh, no!" Nancy protested vigorously. "I won't let you do that! You like to hike so well. Please go on. I'll have a good time all by myself. Really, I will."

"I don't like to leave you, Nancy. But if you insist——"

"I do, Helen. Please don't worry about me. I'll have a good time here. If you don't mind, I may take the launch out while you're gone."

"If you do, you'd better not go far," Helen advised her. "We girls bought it secondhand for a song, and it's my private opinion the engine isn't much good."

"I'll be careful," Nancy promised.

She could scarcely hide her eagerness to be off, but she was forced to wait until Helen and her friends had started on their hike. It seemed to Nancy that they would never leave, but at last they trudged away with their knapsacks slung over their shoulders.

"You'll wish you had gone, too!" Helen called back over her shoulder.

As soon as the girls were out of sight, Nancy hurried down to the launch which was tied to the dock not far from the camp. She examined the engine. She had frequently handled motor boats, but never one of this particular make.

"I believe I can manage it all right, if only I can get the engine started," Nancy told herself.

She discovered a pin sunk in the rim of a flywheel, and after adjusting other parts, pulled it out rather timidly. She gave the wheel a vigorous turn to the right. She tried again, swinging it farther and snapping back hard. To her delight the engine began to roar.

Cutting down the motor, Nancy steered out into deep water. At first she followed the shore, but as she became more familiar with the wheel and as the engine appeared to work perfectly, she headed out into the lake.

Nancy experienced a real thrill as the little launch responded to her hand. The lake was as smooth as glass, and there was scarcely a cloud in the sky. As the launch cut through the water a tiny spray blew in Nancy's face, but she did not mind.

Far ahead she could see the opposite shore, and she headed straight for the point where she knew the Topham bungalow was located.

"If only the caretaker will let me in when

I get there!" she thought, as she drew near her objective point.

But she was doomed never to reach the opposite shore that day, for unexpectedly there was a miss in the steady throb of the engine. The motor gave one long slow wheeze and died.

"Oh, what can have happened to it now?" Nancy cried anxiously. "I can't have run out of gasoline."

An examination of the tank revealed that it was nearly full. Nancy studied the engine doubtfully. Like most girls, she had never interested herself in the mechanics of what made wheels go around.

"Hateful thing!" she murmured. "I believe it stopped on purpose!"

Too late, Nancy recalled that her chum had warned her about the engine. Now, as she glanced toward shore, she saw no hope of rescue. She was within sight of the Topham bungalow, which appeared deserted, but miles from her own camp.

For nearly an hour she worked over the engine, but her efforts were useless. The stubborn motor refused to start.

"I'll have to sit out here all day," Nancy thought miserably. "This means I won't get to visit the Topham cottage after all!"

It was especially tantalizing to be so close

to the bungalow and yet know that she could not reach it. Nancy was tempted to swim, but she gave up the idea almost as quickly as it occurred to her, for she realized that even if she reached the Topham bungalow she would have no means of returning to camp. She decided that it would be better to remain on the lake and wait for a passing boat to rescue her.

Slowly the hours dragged on, and the launch drifted farther and farther from shore. Never had time seemed to pass so monotonously.

"There's one thing certain," Nancy Drew told herself. "If I ever get out of this launch, I'll never set foot in it again!"

The camp boat seemed to be the only one on the lake, and as the day wore on she began to wonder if she ever would be rescued. The sun beat down upon her, and with the passing hours she became hungry as well as uncomfortable.

"After to-day I'll never have another chance to visit the Topham bungalow alone," she thought. "Helen means well, but she will stay with me every minute. I think the best thing I can do is to tell her I am starting for home to-morrow—that is, if I'm ever lucky enough to reach shore. On my way back to River Heights I'll stop at the Topham cottage. Helen will be disappointed, but it can't be helped."

For want of other occupation, Nancy turned

her attention again to the engine. When the sun sank into the water several hours later, she was still bending over it, a determined look in her eyes.

"There!" she muttered as she straightened up. "I've certainly done enough to it. If it won't go now, it never will."

She gave the wheel a vicious swing, and, to her astonishment, the engine began its steady roar as unconcerned as though it had never stopped.

"If that isn't the limit!" Nancy exclaimed in wonder.

Hopefully, she glanced toward the shore, but already shadows were beginning to lurk among the trees and she knew that in less than an hour it would be dark.

"It's too late to visit the bungalow to-night," she decided regretfully. "I'd better get back to camp before this engine changes its mind again."

Obedient to her will, the little launch plowed through the water toward camp, its engine laboring faithfully. As she eased up to the dock, Nancy saw Helen and her friends just trudging into camp. They hailed her with delight.

"I'm nearly dead," Helen announced. "You were smart to stay in camp, Nancy." She stopped abruptly and stared at her chum.

"Why, you're all sunburned, and you're covered with grease! What have you been doing?"

"Taking a sunbath," Nancy laughed. "By the way, Helen, you were right about that engine; but I don't think it will give you any more trouble this summer. Anyway, I've donated eight hours to the cause."

"Eight hours!" Helen gasped. "You've not been out on the lake all that time?"

"It served me right, I guess. I should have gone on the hike."

But while Nancy made light of her adventure, she was disappointed. She had wasted a day, and time was precious. Would she ever reach the Topham bungalow? So far she had been thwarted at every turn.

CHAPTER XIV

An Exciting Discovery

"NANCY DREW, why are you packing that suitcase? You're not leaving camp already?"

Helen Corning, entering the cabin which she shared with Nancy, stopped in the doorway and stared in amazement at her chum, who was folding wearing apparel carefully into her suitcase.

"I'm afraid I must leave this afternoon," Nancy admitted regretfully.

"But you've been here only three days," Helen protested. "Don't you like the camp?"

"Oh, I've had a wonderful time," Nancy cried impulsively. "And the girls have been so nice to me. I'd love to stay, but I can't. There's something important I must attend to at once."

"Can't it wait?"

"I'm afraid not. I've waited too long already."

"But the dance, Nancy! You don't want to miss it."

"I don't want to, Helen; but I really must go this afternoon."

"I can't understand what's made you change your mind so suddenly. It wasn't that horrid experience in the launch, was it?"

Nancy Drew laughed and shook her head. She could not tell Helen her real reason for departing. So long as she remained at camp she knew that Helen and her friends would not leave her alone for a minute. It would be impossible to visit the Topham bungalow on the opposite side of the lake without offering explanations, and Nancy was unwilling to disclose the purpose of her trip.

In spite of Helen's teasing, she remained firm in her decision to leave camp. Directly after luncheon she slung her suitcase into the roadster and took leave of the girls. Regretfully, they watched her go.

"Now, if only I can find my way to the Topham bungalow," Nancy thought.

The previous day she had casually inquired from Helen which road led to the Topham bungalow, but the directions had been rather hazy. Coming to a fork, she selected the left hand road which appeared to circle the lake. As Helen had indicated, it was winding and narrow, and richly sprinkled with sharp rocks.

From camp it was comparatively easy to reach the Topham bungalow by launch, but the distance around the lake was nearly eight miles. Nancy was forced to drive slowly, and had she met another car it would have been difficult to have passed.

In places the road was muddy, for overhanging trees and bushes protected the moist earth from the rays of the sun. The going was especially hard because of two deep ruts which apparently had been made by a heavy truck.

"I wonder what a truck was doing up this road?" Nancy mused somewhat curiously. "The tracks appear to have been made today too."

As she drove along, she noticed a number of summer cottages, but as the season was late nearly all were boarded up. At last she came within sight of a clearing, and through the trees caught a glimpse of the Topham bungalow.

"I hope I'll find the caretaker," she thought. "I'd certainly hate to go back without seeing him."

Not without a feeling of anxiety, she stopped the roadster at the edge of the road. To her surprise, she observed that the tracks made by the truck did not continue further. Apparently, the truck had turned in toward the bungalow. Nancy hurried up the path. As she emerged from among the trees, she stopped short and stared ahead in amazement.

The entire camp was in disorder. The front door of the bungalow had been flung wide open and the side doors were likewise ajar.

An overturned chair had been dropped carelessly on the porch, and a trail of knickknacks stretched from the house to the path. The grass had been trampled, and there were peculiar marks in the soft earth.

"There's something strange about this," Nancy murmured.

Quickly, she bent down to examine the marks which were clearly visible. At a glance she saw that the footprints had been caused by heavy boots and there were long lines evidently caused by dragging boxes and furniture across the lawn.

"I think I'm beginning to see the light," Nancy told herself. "Now I know what that truck was doing on this road. Unquestionably, it was a moving van, and it came here."

Again she examined the imprints in the soft earth.

"These marks couldn't have been made more than an hour ago, at the latest," she decided.

As she hurried on up the path, it appeared to Nancy that the camp was deserted. There was no sign of Jeff Tucker, the colored caretaker in whose care the bungalow had been entrusted.

Reaching the veranda, Nancy knocked loudly

on the door. When there was no response, she
boldly entered.

"What can this mean?" she asked herself
in dismay, as she stared at the sight before her.

The living room was in confusion. Save for
a few pieces, it was bare of furniture. Even
the draperies and curtains had been ripped
from their rods. The rugs were missing, as
was everything else of value.

To Nancy's astonishment she found that with
the exception of one room the entire house had
been ransacked. Only one bedroom had been
left practically untouched, and as she stepped
into it, she noticed that the rug had been rolled
up and securely tied as though in preparation
for moving.

As Nancy gazed at the disorder about her,
she searched her mind for an explanation.
What could it mean?

"It looks like a case of ordinary robbery to
me," she reasoned.

Nancy had frequently read of cases where
the summer homes of wealthy persons had been
stripped of furniture and rugs by unscrupulous robbers who sold the valuables to secondhand dealers and fences. In recent years there
had been a number of thefts in the vicinity of
Moon Lake, and as a protective measure many
of the cottage owners employed caretakers the
year around.

What had become of Jeff Tucker, the colored man who had been left in charge of the Topham bungalow? The place seemed deserted.

Nancy realized that the Topham bungalow, which had been expensively furnished, would offer a rich prize for thieves. Now, as she viewed the evidence, the suspicion which lurked in her mind developed into firm conviction. She was certain that robbers had ransacked the place, carrying off nearly everything of value.

"They must have taken the Crowley clock too," Nancy told herself with a sinking heart. "If they have, I'll never set eyes on it!"

A feeling of desperation came over the girl as she realized that again she had been thwarted. It seemed almost as though a cruel fate had ordained that the mystery of the missing Crowley will should forever remain unsolved.

"It's barely possible the robbers overlooked the clock," Nancy thought hopefully.

She began to look about in nooks and corners of the bungalow. She opened closets and poked about in drawers, but her search was in vain. She found no clock.

As Nancy returned to the bedroom, she regarded it meditatively. Why had the robbers left this one room practically untouched?

Certainly the furniture was as valuable as that which they had taken. Unquestionably, the thieves had intended to strip the room, for they had rolled up the rug.

"I wonder if they heard me coming and were frightened away?" Nancy asked herself. "I didn't see a sign of their truck, and yet I'm sure they couldn't have left here many minutes before I arrived."

As the thought occurred to her, she glanced uneasily over her shoulder. She realized that she was buried in a wilderness some miles from the nearest house, and the knowledge that unscrupulous men were in the vicinity was anything but reassuring.

"What if those robbers should still be around here?" flashed through her mind.

As Nancy Drew listened tensely, the very silence of the empty house was startling. A strange feeling came over her.

She could almost sense that someone was watching her every movement.

CHAPTER XV

A Desperate Situation

"How silly of me to be afraid!" Nancy Drew laughed nervously. "Probably there isn't a person within miles of here!"

As she glanced about the bungalow it was with relief that she assured herself the place was deserted. Yet, for some reason, she was unable to free herself entirely from the feeling that an unseen danger lurked in wait for her. The very walls seemed to smirk and grimace at her and there was an ominous something in the air.

Now that Nancy felt certain that the Crowley clock had been stolen, she was anxious to get away from the Topham bungalow as quickly as possible.

"I'll drive to the nearest town and report the robbery to the police," she decided. "Those men won't be able to travel very fast with a heavy moving van. There's a chance that they may be caught yet."

Having made the decision, Nancy moved toward the front door. Passing a window, she chanced to glance out, and what she saw caused her to pause in sheer fright.

A heavy-set man with a cap pulled low over his eyes was coming up the path toward the house.

For a moment, Nancy Drew was held in a paralysis of fear. She was positive that the man who was coming toward her was one of the members of the robber band.

Only an instant did the girl hesitate. Then she turned and ran back into the bedroom. Too late she saw that she had trapped herself, for this room had no outside door.

Nancy started back toward the living room, but before she had taken half a dozen steps she realized that her escape had been cut off from that direction. The man had reached the veranda steps.

Frantically, she glanced about for a hiding place. The bedroom closet offered the only possible refuge, and with scarcely an instant's hesitation she stepped into it and closed the door behind her.

Nancy was not a minute too soon. Scarcely had she shut the door when she heard the heavy tread of a man's hobnail shoes on the floor. Peeping cautiously out through a tiny crack in the door, she saw a rough-looking man come into the bedroom. His face was cold and cruel.

As he turned toward the closet where she huddled, Nancy Drew held her breath, scarcely daring to breathe naturally lest her presence be detected. Apparently, the man noticed nothing amiss, for his eyes rested only casually on the closet door.

Nancy's hiding place was anything but comfortable. It was dark and musty and old clothing hung from nails. As dust assailed her nostrils, she held a handkerchief to her face lest she sneeze.

"If I sneeze they'll be sure to find me," she told herself. "They'll know well enough it isn't an animal, even a cat."

She felt around and once came close to catching her hand on a sharp nail. Then she felt something soft on a shelf and imagined it was a sleeping cat. She drew back, then felt more cautiously.

"Only an old fur cap," she told herself, in disgust, "and probably full of moths. Gracious, now I feel like sneezing worse than ever!"

She held her hand over her mouth hard and waited in agony. But presently the desire to sneeze passed and Nancy breathed more freely.

When she dared to peep out through the crack a second time, she saw that two other men had come into the room. From their appearance she knew that they must be members of the robber gang. The first man seemed to be their leader, for he proceeded to issue orders.

"Get a move on!" he growled. "We haven't got all day unless we want to be caught. Take that dresser out of here first."

The two men lifted the heavy piece of furniture and started with it to the door. But they did not move swiftly enough to satisfy the leader, and he berated them savagely.

"If you were in such a hurry why didn't you back the van up to the door instead of leaving it hidden in the bushes?" one of the men retorted angrily.

"Yes, and have someone see us from the road!" sneered the leader.

"Well, carry this out yourself if you think it's so light!"

From her hiding place, Nancy Drew watched the men as they deliberately stripped the room of everything valuable. Piece by piece they carried out the furniture, but the girl was given no opportunity to escape, for the leader of the gang remained in the room while the others made the trip to the van.

"Well, I guess we have everything now," the leader muttered at last.

He turned to follow his companions, who already had gone to the truck, but in the doorway paused for a last careful survey of the room.

At that fateful moment there came a muffled sneeze from the closet.

The robber wheeled about. Walking directly to the closet, he flung open the door and exposed poor Nancy, who was crouching in the far corner. Angrily, he jerked her out.

"Spying on us, eh?" he snarled.

Nancy Drew eyed the man defiantly.

"I wasn't spying."

"Then what were you doing in that closet?"

"I came to see the caretaker."

"Looking for him in a funny place, ain't you?" sneered the man.

Nancy realized that she was in a desperate situation. The look on the robber's face frightened her.

"I heard someone coming and I was afraid," she explained lamely.

"Well, it was unhealthy business that brought you here," the man told her sharply. "What did you hear in that closet?" Without giving her an opportunity to answer the question, he added with a scowl: "I warn you this will be the last time you'll ever stick your nose in business that doesn't concern you!"

As Nancy saw the expression on the man's face, there was no mistaking the ugly threat. One glance assured her that she could expect no mercy. The hopelessness of her situation gave her the courage to defy him.

"I didn't hear much, but I saw plenty!" she cried. "You're nothing but a common thief, and if I get the chance I'll turn you and your gang over to the police!"

"If you get the chance—that's good." The robber laughed mirthlessly. "I'll do with you as I did the caretaker."

"The caretaker!" Nancy gasped in horror. "What have you done with him?"

"You'll find out all in good time."

The man held Nancy's wrists in a viselike grip. Her efforts to free herself were of no avail.

"It won't do you any good to try to get away," her captor informed her.

Nancy was desperate. Suddenly, utilizing every ounce of her strength, she gave her imprisoned wrists a quick upward jerk. As the action tore her hands free, she darted for the door.

With a cry of rage, the robber was after her. Almost in one long leap he overtook her, caught her roughly by the arm, and forced her against the wall.

"Not much you don't!" he snarled.

Nancy Drew struggled this way and that. She twisted and squirmed. She kicked and clawed. But she was powerless in the grip of the man.

"Little wildcat! You won't do any more scratching when I get through with you!"

"Let me go!" Nancy cried, struggling harder.

The man half-carried, half-dragged her across the room. Opening the closet door, he flung her roughly inside.

Nancy heard a key turn in the lock. The sliding of a bolt into place followed.

"Now you can starve for all I care!" the man laughed harshly.

Then the steady tramp of his heavy boots across the floor told Nancy Drew that he had left the house.

CHAPTER XVI

LEFT TO STARVE

WHEN the sound of the footsteps had died away, Nancy Drew was overcome with panic. A feeling of desperation came over her. She realized that the robber had dared to carry out his ugly threat. He had locked her in the closet and had left her there to starve.

At first Nancy was too frightened to think logically. She beat frantically upon the door with her fists, but the heavy oak panels did not give.

"Help! Help!" she screamed.

At last, exhausted by her efforts to force the door open, she fell down upon the floor, a dejected, crushed little figure.

"Maybe those men will come back later and let me out," she tried to encourage herself. "Surely, they can't be so heartless as to leave me here to starve."

But even as the thought came to her, she heard the muffled roar of a heavy truck as it passed the Topham bungalow on the way to the road. With a feeling of utter hopelessness,

Nancy heard the van depart. She knew for a certainty the the cruel, hardened rascals were indifferent to her plight. They had abandoned her to a horrible fate.

The house was as silent as a tomb. Although Nancy had little hope that there was anyone within miles of the cottage, she again raised her voice and shouted for help. Her cries echoed through the empty house and seemed to mock her.

"Oh, why didn't I have sense enough to tell Helen Corning where I was going!" she thought miserably. "She believed I was starting for home. The girls will never dream that I came here."

And her father thought that she intended to remain at the camp for a week! He would not become alarmed over her absence until it was too late. Oh, if only she had never left her home in River Heights!

"Someone may find my roadster at the side of the road," Nancy reasoned, "but it isn't very likely. Few persons pass this way so late in the season."

What had become of Jeff Tucker, the caretaker? Certainly she could expect no aid from that quarter. The robber had hinted that he had done away with the old colored man, and, knowing the character of the rascals, it was impossible not to believe the worst.

As the full significance of the situation dawned upon the girl, panic again took possession of her. In a desperate attempt to break down the door, she threw her weight against it again and again. She pounded upon the panels until her fingers were bruised and bleeding.

At last she sank down on the floor to rest and tried to force herself to reason calmly.

"I'm only wasting my strength this way. I must try to think logically. If I don't, I'm lost."

Nancy Drew recalled that she had once read that it was possible to pick a lock with a hairpin. Feeling in her hair, she found a heavy wire one and began to work at the lock. But in the darkness she could not see and she made little progress. After fifteen minutes she gave the task up in disgust.

"It's no use," she decided miserably. "I'm afraid I'll never get out."

She began to think of her father, of Helen Corning, and other dear friends. Would she ever see them again? As despondency claimed Nancy she was dangerously near tears. Resolutely, she tried to shake off the mood.

"This will never do," she told herself sternly. "Surely, there is a way to get out of here. I must keep my head and try to think of something."

After a time, as a new idea occurred to the girl, she began to rummage about in the closet, hoping that by some lucky chance she might find a tool which would help her force the lock of the door. She searched carefully through the pockets of every garment which hung from the hooks. She groped over every inch of the floor.

She found nothing of value, and the cloud of dust which was stirred up made breathing more difficult than before. The closet had become uncomfortably warm by this time.

Then unexpectedly, Nancy's head struck something hard. Quickly investigating, she discovered a narrow wooden rod suspended overhead. Evidently it had once been used for dress and coat hangers as it was fastened to either wall and ran the length of the closet.

"If I could get that rod down, I might be able to use it to break out a panel of the door," Nancy thought hopefully. "It feels strong and it's about the right size."

She tugged at the rod with all her might. To her satisfaction, one side gave. Another hard jerk brought the rod down on her head.

To her bitter disappointment, Nancy found as she examined the rod that it was too long to use as a ram. But after a little experimentation, she discovered that she could press it into service as a wedge.

Inserting it in the crack between the hinges, she threw all of her weight against the rod. At first the door did not budge.

"Archimedes didn't know what he was talking about when he said the world could be moved with a lever," Nancy murmured. "I'd like to see him move this door!"

As she applied steady pressure to the rod a second time, she saw that the hinges were beginning to give. Encouraged, she applied more force.

"It's coming!" she cried.

Once more she threw her weight against the rod. A hinge tore from the casing and the door sagged. It was now easy to insert the wedge, and Nancy knew that success would soon be hers.

Then, just as another hinge gave way, she was startled to hear footsteps. Someone came running into the bedroom, and a heavy body hurled itself against the door of the closet.

The unexpected action stunned Nancy. Could it be that one of the robbers had heard the noise she had made and had returned to make sure that she did not escape? She discarded the theory as quickly as it came to her. The robbers were far too wise to tarry, once their disgraceful work had been accomplished. Then, too, she had heard their moving van leave.

Frantically, Nancy rattled the door knob.

"Oh, you is a caged lion, dis time," a rather unsteady voice remarked. "You is one o' dese tough robber boys, is you? Well, you won't do no mo' pilferrin', 'cause I done got you surrounded."

"Let me out!" Nancy pleaded. "I'm not a robber!"

The sound of a feminine voice coming from the closet nonplussed the man.

"Say, robber boy, is you imitatin' a lady's voice to th'o' me off de scent? If you is, it won't do no good 'cause I's a natural-born, two-legged blood houn'."

Nancy thought of a way to convince him. She let go her longest and loudest feminine scream.

"Dat's enough! Hold yo' siren! I'll let yo' out. Dar ain't a man in de world could make a racket like dat! Dis way out, lady!"

Expectantly, Nancy waited, but the door did not open.

"My Lawdy!" she heard to her horror. "I's done gone and misplaced de key!"

CHAPTER XVII

JEFF TUCKER'S STORY

THERE was another long wait and then, to her relief, Nancy Drew heard a key turn in the lock and then a bolt shot back. Quickly she pushed the closet door open and stepped out into the light.

She stood face to face with Jeff Tucker, the colored caretaker employed by the Tophams. The robbers had led her to believe that they had harmed the old fellow, and Nancy was glad to see him well and happy—albeit a little too happy, for Jeff Tucker plainly had had a bit too much to drink.

Jeff still knew very well what was going on about him, but a certain alcoholic glitter in his eyes and his somewhat unsteady stance informed Nancy that he was not just as sober as the proverbial judge. She suspected that while he had been absent on his convivial celebration, the robbers had made off with the Topham furniture, for even in his condition of semi-inebriety Jeff seemed to realize that something was amiss. He stared at Nancy, then his eyes roved about the topsy-turvy room.

"Say, white gu'l, you tell me wheah all dis heah fu'niture is at!"

Nancy smiled in spite of herself at the old caretaker's bewilderment, for try as he might, he evidently could not rationalize the situation.

"The most definite information I can give you," she said, "is that some robbers carted it away. If you had been here attending to your duty, it would never have happened."

" 'At's right! 'At's right! Blame me! I ain't s'posed to be no standin' ahmy—I's just a plain culled man with a wife and seven chillun a-dependin' on me. No mom! I ain't havin' no truck wit' dem machine-gun boys!"

Jeff paused and passed his hand over his forehead as if he were trying to wipe away the alcoholic cobwebs that were accumulating about his perceptive faculties. Then suddenly he pointed a bony finger at Nancy and demanded:

"How come you heah?"

"That's a fine question for you to ask!" replied Nancy indulgently. "But I don't mind telling you. I arrived just as the robbers were hauling off the last of the furniture. They locked me in the closet. I must have been there for hours."

"You was in dat dah closet all dat time!"

Jeff's voice suddenly took on a pathetic tone. "You po'h chile! Suppose you had o' stahved to death in dah, or da house had burned down, or you was scared into fits, or——"

"There now, Jeff. Don't take on about what might have happened to me. I'm all right."

Nancy determined to try persuasion on the old fellow in order to find out what had happened to him.

"Tell me where you were last night," she suggested gently.

"Well, Miss, it was dis heah way: I was out in dah yard a-chorin' around last night and a-thinkin' how I wished I was some place whah I wasn't—just any place, I didn't mind wheah. I was just all fed up bein' a caih-taker and takin' caih o' all dis truck from mornin' till night. It ain't such an excitin' life, Miss, and while I's done sowed all mah wild oats, I still sows a little rye now and den."

"Yes, Jeff—I can smell that on your breath right now."

Jeff wiped the back of his hand over his mouth in an apparent effort to keep his rye-laden breath from being propagated into the atmosphere.

"You cain't blame me, Miss," he protested. "*He* give it to me."

"Who is this 'he'?"

"Why, dat white man who drives up in de

big see-dan. He sees me out thah and knows how lonesome and useless I feels, so he says: 'Jeff, hop in. I know a place where!' So in I hops. Course I locked up dis heah house and de bahn and seen dat everything was safe."

"Safe! From the looks of this room one could hardly call it that!"

"Oh, well, Miss, it looked safe and I felt safe too when we whizzed off in dat big cah. Den dis white man he says: 'Jeff, how about a little drink?' An' I says, 'I don't mind, seein' it's you.' Den I had one and some mo' too I guess, cause aftah while I didn't feel like I was ridin' in no automobeel at all. I thought dat de chariot had done gone an' swung low an' I was a-bein' wafted off to some place in de gen'ral direction o' heaven!"

"Well, that was a fine thing to do, I must say," Nancy commented. "Then what happened?"

"I comes to. I sees I ain't in no chariot no mo' but I's in a ho-tel. And I's in bed and I's feelin' pow'ful sickish-like and discouraged. Well, I gets my clo'es on and I sees mah keys to de house is done been pilfehed. Den I tries to recollect what done come to pass and I gets s'picious. I says to myself, 'Jeff, how come dat white man so friendly? How come he give you drinks dat costs fo' dollars a pint. How come

you ain't got no keys? Black boy, bestir yo'-
self. And here I is!"

"Oh, yes, you're here all right," Nancy returned severely. "And a fine mess you've
made of it, too. What do you think Mrs. Topham will say when she learns?"

Jeff rolled his eyes.

"Lawdy, Miss! What *will* she say? I reckon
I's done gone and discharged myself."

"It would be only what you deserve, Jeff.
You were unfaithful to your trust."

"What you mean, Miss, trust? I don't trust
nobody no mo'—especially no foot-loose white
boys a-travelin' around in see-dans."

"You don't understand. I mean you didn't
treat Mrs. Topham right in going off."

"I reckon you's right, Miss. Ole Jeff done
gone and made a fool of himself. I realize dat
whatever I gets, I's got it a-comin'."

A tear rolled out on Jeff's black, furrowed
old cheek, and he wiped it away with his handkerchief.

"There, Jeff," Nancy said consolingly.
"Let's forget about what has been done and
think about what we can do to straighten
things out. I'll try to help you. We must report the robbery to the police right away. Is
there a telephone in the house?"

"No, Miss. We ain't got no telephone heah.
We always uses de R. F. D."

"Then we shall have to go to town as quickly as we can in my car. Do you suppose that you would recognize the man who enticed you away, Jeff?"

"Say, would I 'member him? I'd recognize dat man in a bootleggah's convention. He was tall an' slick-lookin' with a kind of a 'gimme' look in his eyes. Yes mom! I suah would know dat baby!"

Before leading the way to her roadster, Nancy Drew thought of the old Crowley clock again and all that it might mean in the solving of the mystery of the will. Jeff, as caretaker, would surely know whether or not it was in the bungalow before the robbery.

"Tell me something, Jeff," she said. "Was there an old clock in the house—a tall, square-faced, mantel clock?"

"Yes, Miss. But all I ever done to it was dust it. I never wound it up to see if it would run. I's got a watch o' my own." Jeff punctuated his remarks by taking a large, silver, open-face watch from his pocket and holding it to his ear. "She's done run down too. I reckon dat I was in dat ho-tel when I should o' been tendin' to dis watch."

"Never mind the watch, Jeff. You're sure there was a clock in the house then?"

"Oh, I's dead rights on dat, Miss. Dar suah was! I recollects dat clock just as plain as day. I wouldn't fohget dat clock. No, mom, never!"

Nancy now felt almost certain that this was the clock which contained the notebook telling of what disposal had been made of the Crowley will and that it had been stolen by the robbers.

She must recover the clock! And there was only one way. The thieves must be apprehended and the stolen good returned. With this thought in her mind, she rushed out toward her roadster, calling to Jeff to follow.

"I's a-comin', Miss," Jeff called. "Just a minute!"

He half-hobbled off behind the house out of Nancy's sight, while she sat waiting impatiently in her roadster. She started the engine and warmed it up, but Jeff still failed to return.

She called to him, but there was no response. Finally, she could stand the suspense no longer. Jumping to the ground, she set off to find out what had become of the old scamp.

She found Jeff leisurely performing an elaborate facial ablution at the cistern pump. He would pump his hands full of water and then, with a great spluttering noise, dash it against his face.

"For goodness's sake, Jeff," said Nancy, provoked, as she came upon him. "Don't you realize I've been waiting for you! Those robbers will probably be in the next state before we even succeed in notifying the police.''

'' 'Scuse me, Miss, but I's takin' a little wash.''

''I see you are. But can't that wait?''

''But dis heah wash is impohtant. I just wants to git good and sober befo' I goes into dat po-lice station, and dis cold water is good fo' what ails me.''

Coax, wheedle or threaten, Nancy was unable to hurry Jeff a minute. But at last he had finished, and Nancy, with a sigh of relief, loaded him into the waiting roadster.

As she stepped upon the accelerator and the car moved slowly out onto the highway, she wondered where the old Crowley clock was now and whether she would ever be able to recover it from the thieves.

CHAPTER XVIII

Notifying the Police

It was probably fortunate for Nancy Drew that the traffic police were not patrolling the road, for as she opened the throttle wider and wider, her roadster responded with a surge of power that sent the car along at breath-taking speed.

"Dis ole bus can suah step," observed Jeff. "'Spose it turns turtle?"

"Don't worry, Jeff. It won't. I know this roadster."

Nancy Drew did know the limit to which she dared go. She guided the car skillfully and in a short time they were entering the outskirts of Melborne, the nearest town to the Topham bungalow.

"Bettah slow down now, Miss," Jeff cautioned. "De marshal of dis town is mighty persnickitty about how folks acts. He's run me in mo'n once."

"For speeding?"

"No, just fo' enjoyin' myself."

"Then I suppose you can tell me where the jail is."

" 'Deed I can, Miss. I suah can! Fact is, dis is my favorite jail. You goes right down Central Avenue to Maple Street and turns to de left, and dar you is."

The roadster stopped in front of the building with a lurch, and Nancy stepped out briskly, with Jeff following at a more leisurely gait.

"I must see an officer," Nancy announced as she entered the office. "I want to report a robbery."

A buzzer rang and soon a marshal, followed by several men, entered. Nancy quickly told them all she know about the Topham robbery, and to corroborate what she had said, she called Jeff for his version.

"She speaks de troof," testified Jeff, " 'cept she don't make it strong enough. First thing dey kidnaps me so I won't be around to raise no ruckus. Den dey gives me some kind of a sleepin' powdah and pahks me in a ho-tel. But I comes to and goes back, and dar I find dis gu'l cooped up in a closet just as she told you. And dey wrecked Mis' Topham's house and stole all de furniture."

The marshal and his men listened attentively, and plied Nancy with questions to clear up certain points.

"Have you any idea which road they took?"
the marshal asked her.

"Yes, sir. I examined the tire tracks where
the thieves had backed a truck up to the house
and noticed the pattern they made in the turf.
When we passed the road-crossing a few miles
out of town, I saw the same tracks just off to
the side of the road where they had slipped off
in turning their truck northward."

"Can you lead the way?"

"Yes, I'll do everything in my power to
help."

The marshal terminated the interview by
giving curt orders to his deputies.

"Get your automobile started," he directed
Nancy. "We'll follow in the police car."

"Hurry!" Nancy begged as she turned toward the door. "Those men have nearly an
hour's start of us now!"

Hastily, she ran to the street and sprang into
the roadster. Starting the motor, she waited
impatiently for the marshal and his men to
appear. After a seemingly interminable wait,
they came out, buckling on holsters.

They piled into the "police car" which stood
at the curbing and the marshal took the wheel.
After several unsuccessful attempts he started
the motor. Jeff Tucker, who had followed the
men from the office, would have inflicted his

person upon the already overburdened car, but as he attempted to gain the running board, he was forced gently but firmly back upon the sidewalk.

"Follow me!" Nancy cried to the marshal.

Shifting gears, she started off down the road. At the corner she looked back to see that the police car was following, and caught a glimpse of Jeff Tucker who stood gazing mournfully after the departing automobiles.

At the edge of town, Nancy selected the road which she felt certain the robbers had taken. Her high-powered roadster was built for speed and several times she was forced to slow down in order that the marshal and his men might keep her in sight.

Nancy had gone perhaps eight or nine miles when unexpectedly she came to a fork in the road. Uncertain which branch-off to take, she brought the roadster to a halt. The police car pulled up alongside.

"What's the matter now?" the marshal called out.

"I don't know which way to go."

The marshal and his deputies sprang from their automobile and began to examine the tracks in the road. But if a moving van had passed that way, the tire marks had been obliterated by other vehicles. There was no clue

to indicate which route the robbers had selected.

"They must have taken the righthand fork,"
the marshal hazarded.

Nancy shook her head doubtfully.

"Doesn't the lefthand road lead to Garwin?"

The marshal nodded.

"Then it strikes me the robbers would have
taken that road. It seems reasonable that they
would head for a large city where they could
dispose of the stolen goods."

"Maybe you're right," the marshal admitted
reluctantly.

"I'll tell you what we'll do," Nancy pro-
posed, as she had an inspiration. "You take
the righthand road and I'll head for Garwin."

"And if you should overtake those rascals,
what would you do?" the marshal demanded in
some amusement. "You couldn't expect to
stop them single-handed."

"I wouldn't try. I'd race back and give the
alarm. Hurry! Every minute that we delay
gives them just that greater advantage!"

Without waiting until the marshal had returned to his automobile, Nancy Drew backed
her car and headed down the lefthand road.
The highway was smooth, and as there was a
clear stretch ahead, she drove rapidly. She
realized that already the robbers had a big

start, and that if once they reached Garwin she could not hope to overtake them.

"I'm sure I'm on the right trail," she told herself. "That other road doesn't lead anywhere in particular."

After she had traveled several miles, Nancy became less confident. Although she had passed a number of side roads, she had kept to the main highway, and she realized that it would have been easy for the moving van to elude pursuit by taking any one of the branches.

"Still, the robbers can't know that they are being followed," she reasoned. "It's likely they'll be off their guard."

Fifteen minutes passed, and Nancy began to fear that after all she had selected the wrong road at the fork. Presently, as she noticed a man with a team of horses approaching, she determined to question him.

"Have you seen a large moving van on this road?" she called out as she stopped the roadster alongside the wagon.

"A truck passed me about twenty minutes ago," the farmer told her. "The big road hog tried to push me into a ditch!"

Highly elated at the information, Nancy thanked the farmer and drove on.

"At the rate I'm going I should overtake the robbers in a few minutes," she thought. "Oh, if only I could get my hands on the Crowley clock before the police confiscate the stolen goods!''

Ten minutes passed and then another ten. As Nancy gazed anxiously down the road she could see no sign of the moving van.

''I've missed them somewhere,'' she decided, in disappointment. ''There's nothing to do but go back.''

Nancy Drew recalled the fact that she had passed a roadhouse less than a mile back, and it occurred to her that possibly the robbers had stopped there.

''I'll go back there and make inquiry,'' she thought. ''I haven't gone by a single cross road since I talked with that farmer, so if the robbers didn't stop at the roadhouse I can't imagine what became of them. If they were on this road I am certain I would have passed them by this time.''

Dusk was approaching, and Nancy Drew knew that if she were ever to find the robbers it must be within the next hour. Skillfully, she turned the roadster around in the road. A few minutes of fast driving brought her within sight of the roadhouse.

The place was of disreputable appearance, and Nancy suspected that it might be a bad resort to visit. It stood back from the road a short distance, and was half-hidden by tall trees. The building was large and rambling, but rather old and sadly in need of paint. A sign on the gate read: "The Black Horse." Beyond the inn, Nancy caught a glimpse of a garage and a large stable.

She did not enter the private driveway which led to the inn, but stopped her car at the side of the road. Before starting to walk toward the roadhouse, she hesitated.

"I don't like to go in there, but there's no other way," she decided.

She walked briskly up the path, glancing about in all directions for a sign of a moving van. The door of the garage was closed as was the door of the barn, and the thought occurred to her that perhaps the robbers had parked their van inside one of the buildings.

As she drew near the inn, Nancy approached cautiously. As she stepped upon the veranda, coarse laughter reached her ears. She tiptoed to a window and peered inside. What she saw caused her to start in surprise.

In a dingy, dimly lighted room, three men were seated about a table, obviously engaged in a drinking orgy. They were the three men who had robbed the Topham bungalow!

CHAPTER XIX

A RISKY UNDERTAKING

"I MUST notify the marshal at once!" Nancy Drew told herself as she recognized the three robbers.

Turning away from the window, she crept noiselessly from the porch and as soon as she was a safe distance from the inn, broke into a run. As she stepped into her roadster, a sudden thought occurred to her.

"Those robbers must have parked their van in the garage back of the inn. If only I could get my hands on the clock before I notify the police! Once the marshal takes charge of the stolen goods, I'll have no opportunity."

Motivated by the impulse, Nancy drove on down the road a short distance, and, rounding a bend, came up on another side road which led into the woods directly behind the inn. Stopping the roadster where it would be hidden by the trees, she got out and hurried through the timber. Before leaving the car, she had secured her flashlight, for already it was growing dark.

155

Cautiously, she approached the inn from the rear. Reaching the garage, she found the doors closed, but investigation disclosed that they had not been locked.

She opened one of the doors and looked inside. There was no sign of a truck—only a battered old Ford car.

"They must have parked the van in the barn," she decided.

As she opened the stable door, it squeaked in an alarming fashion. Anxiously, she glanced toward the inn, but so far as she could tell her actions were unobserved. There was no one in sight.

Flinging the door wide, the girl peered hopefully into the dark interior. A low cry escaped from her lips.

There in front of her stood the moving van!

"What a piece of luck!" she exclaimed, as she viewed the truck which the robbers had left in the barn. "Now if I can only find the clock!"

With a last cautious glance in the direction of the roadhouse, she hastily closed the barn door lest it swing in the wind and attract attention. With the doors shut, the interior of the barn was dark.

As Nancy switched on her automobile flashlight and played it over the moving van, she was disappointed to note that it was a covered one. The rear doors were closed. Nevertheless, although she could not see inside, she was certain the truck contained the goods stolen only a few hours before from the Topham bungalow.

Securing a firm grip on the door handle, she gave it a quick turn. To her surprise, the door did not open.

With an exclamation of disappointment, Nancy turned her flashlight on it and for the first time noticed the keyhole. The robbers had locked the van!

"Oh, dear, now what shall I do?" she questioned frantically. "I'll never be able to break the lock."

Desperately, she glanced about. She dared not remain many minutes in the barn lest the robbers return and find her there. Yet she could not admit defeat.

"Perhaps the keys were left in the ignition switch," she thought hopefully.

She rushed to the front of the van and clambered into the driver's seat. An examination of the dashboard did not reveal the keys hanging from the ignition switch.

"The robbers must have taken the keys with them," she told herself.

Nancy was discouraged. She was on the point of admitting defeat when a thought came to her.

Among her acquaintances there were a number of persons who upon occasion hid their automobile keys under the front seat. It was barely possible that the robbers had done likewise.

Nancy hastily pulled up the leather seat and looked underneath. A ray of her flashlight illuminated a small object in one corner. Eagerly, she snatched it up and saw that it was a key ring.

"Luck was with me once," she murmured, as she ran back to the rear of the van.

After trying several of the keys, she at last found one which would fit the lock. Turning it, she jerked open the door. As she flashed her light about inside the truck she saw that she had made no mistake. The van contained the stolen goods and it was loaded nearly to the top.

"What shall I do if the clock is on the bottom?" Nancy groaned as another problem occurred to her. "I'll never find it."

Dexterously, she swung herself up on the load. She flashed the light about on chairs, tables, rugs and boxes. There was no sign of the Crowley clock.

Then the beam rested for a moment upon an object in a far corner, and with a low cry of delight Nancy saw that her search had been rewarded. Protected by a blanket, an old fashioned mantel clock rested on top of a center table in the very front of the van!

She scrambled laboriously over odd pieces of furniture as she tried to reach the clock. Her dress caught on something sharp and tore, but Nancy did not heed it. She snatched at the blanket and swept the clock toward her.

One glance at the timepiece assured her that it fit the description Abigail Rowen had given her. It had a square face and the top was ornamented with a crescent. Nancy was almost certain that it was the Crowley clock.

But as she stood staring at it, her keen ears detected the sound of voices outside the barn. The robbers were coming back!

"I'm lost!" flashed through her mind.

Clutching the blanket and the clock tightly in her arms, Nancy Drew partly crawled and partly fell over objects as she struggled to get out of the truck before it was too late. She was afraid to think what would happen to her if the robbers discovered her in the van.

Reaching the door, she leaped lightly to the floor. She could now hear heavy footsteps coming closer and closer.

Nancy slammed the truck doors shut and searched wildly for the keys.

"Oh, what did I do with them?" she thought frantically.

She saw that they had fallen from the door

to the floor and snatched them up. Hurriedly inserting the right key in the lock, she secured the doors.

The deed was not accomplished a minute too soon. As Nancy wheeled about she distinctly heard the murmur of angry voices outside. The robbers were quarreling among themselves, and already someone was working at the fastening of the barn door.

Escape was cut off. Nancy felt that she was cornered.

"Oh, what shall I do?" she thought in despair.

CHAPTER XX

WHAT NANCY FOUND

WHILE Nancy Drew hesitated, uncertain which way to turn, her mind worked more clearly than ever before.

She realized instantly that she could not hope to run to the front of the car and place the keys under the seat where she had found them. Instead of attempting the impossible, she flung them upon the floor.

Then glancing frantically about for a hiding place, she saw an empty manger. Running to it, she scrambled inside and dropped the blanket over her head just as one of the barn doors swung open.

Three men came in, closing the door after them, and, as Nancy had suspected, they were the robbers. Evidently, they had been drinking, for they were quarreling among themselves over the division of spoils.

"Aw, shut up," the leader growled. "Get in and let's be getting out of here before we have the cops down on our heads."

Nancy heard him rummaging under the seat of the car.

"Say, what did you do with them keys?" he demanded harshly of one of his men.

"What do you suppose?" came the unpleasant response. "I put 'em under the seat."

"Then come and find them, and don't be all day about it, either!"

"All right. Get out of the way and give me a chance!"

As the second robber went to the truck and began a careful search for the keys, Nancy Drew crouched fearfully in her hiding place.

"I don't see what could have happened to them keys," the robber complained after an unsuccessful search. "I put 'em right under this seat."

"Say, if you've lost 'em—" the leader did not finish the threat, for at that moment the third robber stooped over and picked up something at his feet.

"Here they are on the floor! You must have put 'em in your pocket and dropped 'em out."

"I didn't!" the other retorted. "I never had them keys in my pocket."

The robbers were in a quarrelsome mood and would have engaged in a battle then and there had not the leader interposed.

"Say, cut out the comedy! We ain't got no

time for a fight unless we want to land behind
the bars!"

"And if we do, it will be your fault!   You
left that girl to starve——"

"Shut up!" the leader snarled. He rattled
the rear door of the van and found it locked.
"There's no harm done this time. No one has
meddled with the truck. Now get in before I
give you a swift kick!"

After a few more angry words, the three
robbers climbed into the front seat and started
the engine. Due to their inebriated condition
they had overlooked the barn doors, and before the van could be backed from the building, it was necessary for one of the men to get
out and fasten them back.

In relief Nancy watched the men go. The
moment they were a safe distance from the
barn, she scrambled out of the manger.

She paused long enough to make certain that
the van had taken the road to Garwin. Then,
clutching the precious clock in her arms, she
turned and ran.

As Nancy darted into the woods, she cast
an anxious glance over her shoulder, but to
her intense relief she saw that she was not
being followed. There was no one to be seen
in the vicinity of the roadhouse, and the big
moving van was proceeding slowly on its way

toward Garwin, the occupants oblivious that their whereabouts had been discovered.

"I had a narrow escape that time," Nancy told herself as she ran. "I hate to think of my fate if I had been discovered." She chuckled softly at her own bravado and clutched the mantel clock more tightly in her arms. "Oh, well, it was worth the risk I took!"

It was dark in the woods and Nancy could see only a few feet ahead of her. To her chagrin she discovered that she had left her automobile flashlight somewhere in the barn, probably in the manger. There was no time to go back after it. Confident that her sense of direction was good, she plunged through the bushes toward the place where she had parked her roadster.

"I'm sure the clock is the right one," she thought. "Now, if it only contains Josiah Crowley's notebook!"

In the timber there was insufficient light for her to examine the clock, but from the hasty glance she had given it in the barn, she was almost certain it was the timepiece Abigail Rowen had described to her. If the old woman's story was correct, she would find Josiah Crowley's notebook inside.

Reaching the roadster and finding it exactly as she had left it, the girl sprang inside.

"I'll go for the police as fast as I can and

send them after the robbers," she decided.
"The Tophams don't deserve any consideration, but I couldn't be mean enough to sit
quietly by and let them lose their household
goods."

Then, as she was about to start the motor,
her glance fell upon the Crowley clock which
she had placed on the seat beside her. She
was fairly overcome with curiosity to learn
what it would reveal. As she hesitated, she
found it impossible to resist the temptation of
investigating it immediately, even at the cost
of a few minutes delay.

Impulsively, she opened the glass door and
ran her hand around the walls. There was
nothing inside.

"Gone!" Nancy groaned.

Could it be that the Tophams had discovered
the notebook only to destroy it? Nancy discarded the thought as quickly as it came to
mind, for she recalled the conversation she had
overheard between Ada and Isabel. No, they
were as ignorant as herself concerning the
location of the will.

It was more likely that Abigail Rowen had
been confused in her story. After all, she had
not declared that the notebook would be found
inside the clock. Nancy had made the deduc-
tion herself.

"I was almost certain I'd find the notebook," she murmured in disappointment. "It must be here somewhere."

Turning the clock upside down, she gave it a hard shake. Something rattled. Hopefully, she repeated the action. Unquestionably, there was something bulky inside.

"It must be the notebook!" Nancy thought in excitement. "Unless I'm wrong, it's behind the face! How can I get it off?"

After a vain attempt to remove the heavy cardboard face with her fingers, she lifted the automobile seat and found a small tool with which she could pry. It then required but an instant to remove the two hands of the clock and jerk off the face.

As the cardboard fell to the floor, Nancy peered hopefully inside and gave a low cry of delight.

"Eureka!"

There, at one side of the clock, attached to a hook in the top, dangled a tiny blue notebook!

CHAPTER XXI

CAPTURING THE ROBBERS

EAGERLY, Nancy Drew tore the little note-book from the hook. The light was dim, but by holding the book directly under the dash-light, she could make out the words on the cover: "The Property of Josiah Crowley."

"I've found it at last!" she cried.

Quickly turning the first few pages, she saw that they were yellowed with age. The writing was fine and cramped, and the ink had faded. These pages were crowded with business no-tations, but in the poor light it was next to im-possible to make out the words.

Nancy was excited, for she was positive that the notebook would disclose what Josiah Crow-ley had done with his will. Yet, she realized that she could not hope to read through the book without a considerable loss of precious time. If she were to report the whereabouts of the robbers to the police, she must not delay another instant.

"I'll read the notebook later," she decided. Hurriedly replacing it on the hook inside the clock, she tacked on the face again. Then dropping the timepiece on the seat beside her, she covered it with a blanket.

Starting the engine, she skillfully backed the roadster and headed for the main road. Reaching the highway, she cast an anxious glance in the direction the robbers had taken. There was no sign of a light on the road. The moving van had disappeared.

"I must travel some now," Nancy told herself grimly. "Those robbers have at least ten minutes start, and I may have trouble finding the marshal and his deputies."

Bending low over the steering wheel, she deliberately stepped hard on the accelerator. The roadster leaped forward as though it, too, comprehended the need for haste.

"If those men reach Garwin before the marshal overtakes them, there won't be one chance in a hundred of capturing them," Nancy thought. "It was foolish of me to take time to look at the clock."

Presently reaching the fork in the road, she selected the right hand turn, and with undiminished speed rushed on. She had gone several miles beyond the fork when far ahead she caught sight of an automobile headlight. Nancy promptly reduced the speed of the car.

"The marshal and his deputies may have

given up the search and are coming back," she reasoned. "I must be careful not to pass them."

As the automobile approached, Nancy slowed her roadster practically to a standstill. Then as she recognized the police car, she brought her own automobile to a halt. As the marshal and his deputies flashed by, she cried out for them to stop.

There was a loud screeching of brakes as the police car came to an abrupt halt. Springing from the roadster, Nancy ran forward.

"Quick!" she called to the marshal. "The robbers have taken the road to Garwin! If you hurry you can overtake them! Go on and I'll follow!"

Without waiting for more, the marshal and his deputies drove off at top speed. The automobile rounded a bend and was lost to view.

For an instant Nancy Drew stood looking after it. Then, springing into her roadster, she, too, was off.

Following close behind the police car, the girl sped down the road in pursuit of the robbers. The two automobiles passed the roadhouse beyond the fork and raced toward Garwin.

"We should have overtaken the robbers by this time," Nancy told herself anxiously, after a number of miles had been traversed and still there was no sight of a moving van. "They can't have gone very far."

Ten minutes passed. Then, unexpectedly, she caught a glimpse of a red tail light on the road far ahead.

"It must be the van!" Nancy thought. "The light doesn't appear to be moving fast enough for an automobile."

Evidently, the marshal and his deputies were of the same opinion, for at that moment the police car slowed down.

"Don't fire unless it's necessary," the marshal ordered his men. "But if they resist, pepper them!"

Cautiously, the police car approached. As the headlight played upon the rear of the van, Nancy saw the license plate clearly and recognized the numbers.

Then as the van pulled over to the side of the road, the police car drove alongside.

"Halt!" came the order.

The van did not stop. Instead, it put on additional speed and crowded the police car toward the ditch. Nancy's heart was in her mouth as she watched, for it seemed certain that the marshal and his deputies were doomed.

At the very edge of the road, the police car

by a sudden spurt of speed forged ahead and averted disaster.

"Halt!" rang out the warning cry a second time. "Halt or we'll fire!"

There was a sharp crack of a revolver as the robbers fired the first shot.

The marshal and his deputies answered with a quick volley. One of the shots found its mark—the front tire. The van swerved in the road, and as the two side wheels went off into a steep ditch, toppled over.

In an instant the marshal and his men were out of the police car and had covered the three robbers. So easily had the van tipped on its side that the men were not injured, but the unexpected jar had thrown them off their guard.

"Take their guns!" the marshal ordered.

A deputy relieved the three men of their revolvers and searched their pockets for other dangerous weapons. Another deputy handcuffed them.

By this time Nancy, who had stopped her roadster at the side of the road, reached the scene. As she came running up, the marshal turned to her.

"Can you identify these men?"

As a light was flashed upon each of the robbers in turn, Nancy nodded.

"There is the man who locked me up and left

me to starve," she declared, pointing to the leader of the robber band. "And the stolen goods are in the van."

"They'll get ten or twenty years for this," the marshal promised. "We'll hold them on several charges. You are willing to testify against them, I suppose?"

"Yes, if it is necessary," Nancy promised reluctantly. "But I don't live in this county and I'm anxious to get home right away. It seems to me you have enough evidence to convict them."

"Well, if you don't want to I guess there's no need for you to go back with us," the marshal admitted. "I'll take your address and if your testimony should be required later I'll get in touch with you."

As Nancy told the marshal her name and address, he glanced at her with new interest.

"So you're the daughter of Carson Drew! I see you're following in his footsteps. Starting in young, aren't you?"

Nancy laughed.

"It was only an accident that took me to the Topham bungalow at the critical moment," she protested modestly. "I don't deserve any credit for the round-up."

"Not many girls would have used their brains the way you did," the marshal observed. "Unless I'm mistaken, these robbers are old hands at the game. They have been plying their trade around Moon Lake for a number of seasons. The residents will be mighty grateful for what you've done. And that Mrs. Topham you spoke of—she ought to give you a liberal reward for saving her household goods.''

Nancy shook her head.

"I don't want a reward."

"Just the same you've earned one," the marshal insisted. "If you're shy about blowing your own horn, I'll take it up with this Mrs. Topham myself."

"You don't know her as well as I do," Nancy remarked. "She'll not offer a reward, and even if she did I wouldn't accept it. In fact, I must ask you not to mention my name to her at all."

"You don't want any credit for capturing the robbers?" the marshal gasped in astonishment.

"No, I would prefer that my name not be mentioned in connection with the affair. I have a particular reason for making the request."

"Well, you're a queer one," the marshal remarked. "You're the first person I ever saw who didn't want to take all the glory that was coming to him."

"You'll not mention my name?"

"No, I'll keep it mum," the marshal promised. "And if you're anxious not to figure in the case, I guess we can get along without your testimony." He turned toward the moving van. "I'll just have a look inside and see if everything is here."

Taking the keys which one of the deputies had turned over to him, the marshal unlocked the rear doors of the van and carelessly glanced inside.

"It's all here," he announced.

Nancy smiled and thought of the clock which at the moment was hidden under a blanket in her roadster less than a dozen yards away.

"Let's be getting away from here," the marshal directed briskly. He singled out one of the deputies. "You stay here and guard the stolen goods until we can send another truck after it. I'll see to it that these robbers land behind bars, and then I'll come back."

"Just a minute," Nancy interposed as the marshal was about to escort the three robbers to the police car. "I want to ask a few questions."

She turned to the leader of the robbers.

"It was you who stole the keys from Jeff Tucker after getting him drunk, wasn't it?"

"What if I did?" the robber growled. "I wish I'd finished him!"

Unceremoniously, the three prisoners were crowded into the police car. One of the depu-

ties took the steering wheel and another stood
on the running board, covering the robbers
with his revolver. There was no room left for
the marshal.

"Are you going back through town?" he
asked Nancy.

"Yes, it's right on my way to River
Heights," she responded without a thought as
to the purpose of the question.

"Then if you don't mind I'll ride back with
you. There isn't room in the police car."

"Why—why, of course," Nancy stammered.

At once she thought of the clock which she
had left on the seat of the roadster. What if
the marshal should discover it?

Even as the thought came to her, the marshal started toward the roadster.

CHAPTER XXII

What the Notebook Revealed

"Just—a—minute," Nancy Drew stammered as she darted toward the roadster, blocking the marshal's path. "There's a package in the seat. I'll put it in the back."

Hastily, she picked up the clock which was covered with a blanket.

"Never mind that," the marshal interposed. "I can hold it."

"Oh, it's no trouble to put it in the catch-all at the back," Nancy assured him. "Then it will be out of your way."

Before the man could offer to do it for her, she had carried the clock to the rear of the car. Lifting the cover, she placed it on the floor.

During the ride back to town Nancy Drew was anything but easy in her mind, but she gave no indication that she was nervous. It was not until she had said good-bye to the marshal at the jail that she felt entirely safe.

"That was a narrow escape," she laughed, as she drove away. "It might not have gone so well with me if the marshal had discovered stolen goods in my car. It certainly wouldn't have been easy to explain how I came by that clock.''

Although it was late, Nancy was determined to return to River Heights that night. She was anxious to examine the notebook and learn whether or not it would disclose the hiding place of Josiah Crowley's second will.

"Oh, I'm so eager to get home and have a chance to dig into the notebook!" she thought as she drove along the road. "I went through a lot to get it and I'll be disappointed if it doesn't contain good news. It will mean so much to the Horner girls and poor old Abigail if the will is found.''

It was nearly ten o'clock that night when Nancy, tired and worn from the long automobile ride, reached her home in River Heights. As she drove into the double garage, she noticed that her father's car was gone. A glance at the house disclosed that the windows were dark.

"I wonder where father can be?" she questioned herself. "I wanted to tell him about my discovery right away.''

She removed the Crowley clock from the back of the roadster and paused an instant to gloat over it. She was well satisfied with the result of her detective work.

Locking the garage door, she went inside

and switched on the electric light. The house seemed deserted, for Hannah, the maid, had already retired.

"Father is probably working late at the office," Nancy decided. "Oh, well, I may as well stay up. And while I'm waiting I'll have a look at the notebook!"

During the long ride from Moon Lake she had been impatient for an opportunity to examine the Crowley notebook, and now she lost no time in finding a screwdriver. She took off the face of the clock, and from the hook removed the notebook.

"Now to find what became of the will," she declared, as she curled up in a comfortable chair near a reading lamp. "Oh, I hope everything turns out right for Allie and Grace and for Abigail Rowen!"

Carefully, Nancy thumbed over the pages for they were yellowed with age and she was afraid they might tear. Evidently, Josiah Crowley had used the same notebook for many years.

Page after page the girl read, perusing inconsequential memoranda and numerous notations of property owned by Josiah Crowley, as well as various business transactions made by him. Nancy was surprised at the list of stocks, bonds, and notes which apparently belonged to the estate.   The amount reached well over three hundred thousand dollars.

"I had no idea Josiah Crowley had that much money," she murmured.

After a time she grew impatient of the seemingly endless list, and skipping many pages, turned ahead.

Suddenly, the phrase, "my will," caught and held her attention.   Eagerly, Nancy pounced upon it and began to read.

"I've found it at last!" she told herself in excitement.

The notation was brief and written in Josiah Crowley's cramped hand.

"To whom it may concern: My last will and testament will be found in safety deposit box number 148 in the Masonville National Bank. The box is under the name of Josiah Harkston."

The date of this entry was recent and the ink had not faded as in the earlier entries in the notebook.

"Then there was another will!" Nancy exclaimed aloud.   "Oh, I'm sure it must be in favor of the Horner girls, too!"

She hurriedly read on, but although she carefully examined every page in the book, there was no other mention of the will.

"No wonder the will never came to light," Nancy mused. "Who would have ever thought of looking for it in a safety deposit box under the name of Josiah Harkston? In his zest for safety, Josiah Crowley nearly defeated his own purpose."

Her thoughts were interrupted as she heard an automobile turning in at the drive. Rushing to the window, Nancy saw her father drive into the garage. As he opened the front door she ran to meet him.

"Why, hello, Nancy," he greeted her in surprise. "If I had known you were here, I'd have come home sooner. I was doing some special work on a case. Back from Moon Lake early, aren't you?"

"Yes," Nancy admitted, trying to hide her excitement. "But for a good reason."

Before her father could remove his hat, she plunged into the story of her adventures and ended by showing him the notebook which she had found inside the mantel clock. When she had finished, Carson Drew stared at her with mingled pride and amusement.

"You're a regular detective, Nancy."

"You're making fun of me."

Carson Drew's face sobered.

"No, I'm proud of what you've done, Nancy. I couldn't have done better myself—perhaps not so well. You took a real risk when you encountered those robbers, but so long as you are back home safe and sound, it doesn't matter."

"The Tophams aren't going to thank me when they find out what I have done."

"Hardly. They may accuse you of stealing their clock, although so long as their house was open when you entered they can't claim that you broke in. However, if we can manage to keep the knowledge from them, it will be just as well that they don't learn the details of how the will was found."

Carson Drew picked up the notebook and glanced through it with interest.

"The fortune will make a nice nest egg for someone," he commented, as he looked over the lists of stocks and bonds owned by Crowley. "These securities are of the best, too. All gilt edge."

"I hope the Tophams will be cut off without a cent," Nancy declared.

"It's likely they will be; but of course you never can be certain until the will is read. Unless I am mistaken, your discovery will strike the Tophams at an especially awkward time."

"What do you mean?"

"Well, there's a rumor going the rounds to the effect that Richard Topham has been losing heavily in the stock market this last month. He has been getting credit at a number of the banks on the strength of the inheritance, and I suspect he is depending on Crowley's money to pull him through a tight place. At least he has made every effort to speed up the settlement of the estate."

"It would serve the Tophams right if they lose everything," Nancy said decisively. "They never had a particle of charity for anyone. They would let their relatives starve before they would help them."

Carson Drew glanced again at the notebook in his hand.

"Now that you have found this, the thing to do is locate the will at once before Richard Topham gets wind of what is up," he advised. "We want to administer the *coup de grâce* before the Tophams have a chance to get the fortune into their hands. Once the estate is settled, it will not be easy to wrest it away from them."

"I'd like to turn the matter over to you," Nancy responded promptly. "I'm not familiar with legal procedure and you know exactly what should be done."

"I'll be glad to help you if I can, Nancy. The first thing of course is to get our hands on the will."

"That should be easy. We can drive over to the Masonville National Bank the first thing in the morning."

"Yes, but we haven't authority to open the safety deposit box. It may be necessary to get a court order," Carson Drew reminded his daughter.

"That's so. I hadn't thought of that. But you can manage it, can't you?"

Carson Drew chuckled.

"Well, I know the judge. Yes, I think I can arrange it all right. I'll tell him I am acting as counsel for the Horner girls. I really am, because I promised I'd help them if I could."

"I'm sure everything is going to turn out just as I hoped!" Nancy cried enthusiastically. "The deserving relatives will get the money and the Tophams will be left out in the cold! Abigail Rowen will be able to have the medical attention she needs, and Allie and Grace will be fixed for life!"

"Don't build your hopes too high," Carson Drew advised her wisely. "There may be a slip, you know. We may fail to find the will in the deposit box, and of course there is a chance that Josiah Crowley didn't dispose of the fortune as it was expected that he would. If I were you I wouldn't say anything to the Horner girls until we are certain."

"I won't," Nancy promised, as she turned toward the stairs. "But I can't help hoping. I'm going to bed now and get a good night's rest. Then to-morrow we'll start off on the big adventure! Oh, I can scarcely wait to find out what the will contains!''

Half way up the stairs, she hesitated and then returned to the living room and picked up the notebook which rested on the table.

"After all I've gone through to get my hands on this, I'm not going to take any chances!'' she laughed. ''To-night I'm going to sleep with it under my pillow!''

CHAPTER XXIII

LOOKING FOR THE WILL

WHEN Nancy Drew awoke the following morning, the bright sunlight was streaming in at her open bedroom window. As her eyes turned toward the little clock on her dresser, she was alarmed to see that it was after nine o'clock.

"How could I oversleep on a morning like this?" she asked herself.

Quickly running her hand under the pillow, she brought out the Crowley notebook and surveyed it with satisfaction.

"Oh, what a surprise the Tophams are going to get!" she chuckled softly.

Hastily dressing, Nancy hurried downstairs. She found that her father had already left for the office.

"Oh, dear," she thought. "I wonder if he forgot?"

At that moment Hannah appeared from the kitchen bearing a plate of crisp, steaming waffles.

"Your father said I was to tell you to go to

his office just as soon as you finish your breakfast,'' she informed Nancy. ''He said you were
to bring your notebook.''

''My notebook— Oh, yes, I know what he
meant! It won't take long to eat breakfast,''
she predicted, as she seated herself at the table.

After a hasty meal, she climbed into the roadster and drove to her father's office. She found
him alone in the inner office.

''I'm sorry I overslept this morning,'' Nancy
apologized. ''Have I kept you waiting?''

''Not at all,'' her father assured her pleasantly. ''I told Hannah not to awaken you because I knew you needed rest after your hard
day yesterday. And, anyway, we couldn't do
anything about the will without an order from
the court.''

''Did you get it?''

''Yes, I saw the judge early this morning.
After explaining everything to him he gave me
the paper. I have it here.'' Carson Drew
tapped an inside pocket.

''I brought the notebook with me. You
wanted it, didn't you?''

''Yes, I thought it might be necessary to
show it to the judge, but we won't need it now.
However, it may be well to put it in the safe.
I'll do it now.''

Carson Drew took the notebook from Nancy

and after placing it inside a small safe closed and locked the door.

"When shall we start for Masonville?" Nancy asked somewhat impatiently.

"Right now if you are ready."

After leaving a number of instructions with his private secretary, Carson Drew followed his daughter from the office. He took his place beside her in the roadster.

"I'll never get over it if we don't find the will," she declared, as they drove along. A flush of excitement had tinted her cheeks and her eyes were bright.

"You must remember one thing, Nancy," returned her father calmly. "Crowley was a queer character and did things in a queer way. So the will may be there, and again it may not be. Perhaps he left only further directions in a box. I remember one case in Canada many years ago. An eccentric Frenchman died and he left directions to look in a trunk of old clothes. In the pocket of a coat were found further directions to look in a closet of his home. There his family found directions to look in a copper boiler. The boiler had disappeared and was finally located in a curiosity shop. Inside, on the bottom, was pasted what proved to be a word puzzle. The old Frenchman's heirs were about to give up in despair when a puzzler solved the puzzle and the man's bag of gold was found—under a board in his bedroom!"

"Oh, but they found it, anyway," breathed Nancy.

The trip to Masonville was quickly accomplished, and in a short time Nancy stopped the roadster in front of the Masonville National Bank.

"You may as well come, too," Carson Drew said, as Nancy hesitated.

Parking the car at the curbing, the two entered the bank. Mr. Drew offered his professional card and asked to see the president. After a few minutes' wait, they were ushered into a private conference room. An elderly man arose to greet them.

The introductions accomplished, Mr. Drew hastened to state his mission. Before he could finish the story, the bank president cut him short.

"I am afraid you have come to the wrong place. To my knowledge we have never had dealings with a man by the name of Josiah Crowley."

"Perhaps you did not know him by that name. I believe he had a deposit box here under the name of Josiah Harkston."

"Josiah Harkston?" the banker repeated thoughtfully. "It seems to me we have been trying to get in touch with a man by that name.

If I remember correctly the rent on his safety deposit box has not been paid for some time. If you will wait a moment I will find out."

The banker left the room. He returned in a few minutes with a sheet of paper in his hand.

"According to our record a Josiah Harkston rented box 148 from us, but the past year the rent has not been paid. Here is his signature if you care to look at it."

Eagerly Nancy and her father examined the sheet of paper which the banker handed them. At a glance they saw that the writing was in the cramped hand of Josiah Crowley.

"It may be that Crowley and Harkston were the same person, as you say," the banker continued. "But we have no authority to permit you to examine the contents of the safety deposit box."

"I have an order from the court," Mr. Drew said quietly.

"Oh, that is different." The banker's attitude underwent a sudden change. "May I see the document please?"

"Certainly."

Mr. Drew removed the paper from his pocket and handed it to the banker. After examining it for a minute, the president returned it.

"You find it satisfactory?" Mr. Drew asked.

"Perfectly. You are welcome to open the safety deposit box—of course in the presence of a bank official. I suppose you have the key?"

Nancy's face fell. She had never once thought of the key.

"We have no key," Mr. Drew admitted. "Isn't there one in the bank which will fit the box?" He knew some small banks had this.

"No, we did away with that when we got our regular vault," said the banker. "But— wait a minute," he added suddenly. "I think I can help you out."

He disappeared into another part of the bank and presently came back holding up a sealed envelope.

"That man had two keys for his box and he left one here in my possession, sealed up as you can see. As you have a court order I feel you are entitled to this key," and he handed the envelope to Mr. Drew.

The envelope was marked with Josiah Crow-ley's assumed name, also the number of his box. It contained a small, flat key, nothing more.

"Now we will go to the boxes," said the bank official.

Nancy and her father followed the president into the main part of the bank. They were then admitted into a small room which was pro-tected by heavily barred doors. Finally, they entered the vault which contained the safety deposit boxes.

The president inserted a small key in a lock, then used the key given to Mr. Drew and finally pulled out a metal box which bore the number 148. Politely, he handed the box to Mr. Drew, who quickly lifted the lid and peered inside. Unable to resist the temptation, Nancy peeped over her father's shoulder.

The box was empty save for one document in the bottom.

"Oh, it must be the will!" Nancy cried before Mr. Drew could examine the paper.

"It is the will," her father announced, after a hasty glance at the document.

"A will, eh?" said the bank official, with keen interest.

"Yes, and I will ask you to do me a favor. Kindly place your initials on each page—so you can later on identify it if necessary—and I will do the same."

"Certainly, Mr. Drew. I've done that before."

Mr. Drew thanked the president for the help he had given, and with Nancy left the bank. Once they had gained the comparative privacy of the roadster, they grinned at each other like two mischievous youngsters.

"Well, we put it over, eh, Nancy?"

"We certainly did. But read the will! I'm dying to find out what it says. I can't stand the suspense another minute!"

The will comprised several pages, all written in Josiah Crowley's cramped style. Mr. Drew spread the pages out before him, and Nancy pored over them. Not only was the fine writing difficult to make out, but the legal terms were confusing.

"It's going to be a terrible task to study it all out," Nancy complained.

"Yes, I think we had better take it to the office," Mr. Drew suggested. He picked up the last page of the will and studied it closely. "I see Doctor Nesbitt signed as a witness. No wonder the will never came to light. If you remember, he died a few days after Crowley. Thomas Wackley, the other witness, I never heard of."

"Oh, I don't care who witnessed the will," Nancy said impatiently. "I want to find out if Allie and Grace and poor Abigail got anything. I can't make head nor tale out of it."

"I see their names are mentioned," Mr. Drew told her, pointing to one of the pages.

"Oh, I'm so glad! So long as I know they're taken care of I suppose I can wait until we get to your office to find out the details. We can have the will copied in typewriting."

"Yes, I want to go over the document carefully. It is evident that Crowley drew it up himself, and I want to make certain it is legal."

"Oh, do you think there is any danger it won't be?" Nancy questioned anxiously.

"I can't tell until I go over it in detail, Nancy. But from a hasty examination it appears that the Tophams aren't mentioned, and they are certain to make trouble if they can. I want to make sure there is no way for them to break the will before I notify them we have it in our possession."

Mr. Drew folded the papers and placed them carefully in his pocket. As Nancy started the motor in preparation for the return trip to River Heights she began to chuckle.

"If the will does prove to be legal, won't it be a blow for the Tophams? I'd give a lot to see how they take it. I think it would be a splendid idea to call a meeting of all the relatives and read the will aloud!"

"I'm afraid you have a dark motive behind that idea," Mr. Drew laughed. "But I'll try to humor you this time. What's more, I'll promise that you may be present when the *coup de grâce* is administered to the Tophams!"

CHAPTER XXIV

The Coup de Grâce

"Oh, father, it's nearly two o'clock now. The relatives should be coming in a few minutes! I'm so excited!"

Carson Drew, who stood in the living room of the Drew home smiled indulgently at his daughter as she fluttered about, arranging chairs.

"I believe you're more thrilled than if you were inheriting the fortune yourself," he remarked.

"I am thrilled," Nancy admitted. "I can scarcely wait until the will is read aloud. Won't everyone be surprised? Especially the Tophams. Do you think they will come?"

"Oh, yes, the Tophams will be here. And, unless I am mistaken, they will bring a lawyer with them. Just as soon as they learned that another will had come to light, they began to worry."

"Are you certain the will can't be broken?" Nancy inquired anxiously.

"Of course I can't be certain, Nancy. But I

194

have gone over it carefully, and so far as I can
tell it is technically perfect. Josiah Crowley
was peculiar in some ways, but he was no one's
fool. I'll promise you the Tophams will have
a difficult time of it if they try to break the
will."

After locating the Crowley will in a safety
deposit box at the Masonville National Bank in
the town of Masonville, Carson Drew and his
daughter had read it carefully. Without dis-
closing the contents to anyone, they had called
a special meeting of the relatives at the Drew
home.

With the exception of Abigail Rowen, who
was confined to her bed, all had promised to be
present. Grace and Allie Horner, although not
relatives, had also been invited to attend the
meeting.

"It's too bad Abigail Rowan can't come,"
said Nancy. "But we'll get the news to her
fast enough."

"It will probably be a great surprise all
around," said her father, with a little smile.
"Nancy, you have done a remarkable piece of
work."

"Oh, I can hardly wait to have it all cleared
up," cried the happy girl.

"We may have some hard minutes with the
Tophams, Nancy."

"Yes, I suppose so. I suppose anybody

would be sorry to see a fortune slipping away."

"Well, we'll see what happens," returned the lawyer.

"The Horner girls are coming up the walk now," Nancy announced, glancing out of the window. "I'm dying to tell them the news, but I'll wait."

She greeted Allie and Grace cordially and escorted them to comfortable chairs in the living room.

"Is it true the will has been found?" Allie whispered.

"You and Grace have no cause to worry," Nancy assured her, with a mysterious smile.

No sooner had she seated the Horner sisters than the doorbell rang again. This time she admitted Edna and Matilda Turner, who were dressed in their best black silk gowns. A few minutes later, the Mathews brothers, William and Fred, arrived.

"I guess everyone is here now except the Tophams," Carson Drew commented. "We had better wait for them a few minutes."

There was no need to wait, for at that moment the doorbell jangled sharply. Nancy opened the door and the four members of the Topham family sailed grandly in. As Carson Drew had predicted, they were accompanied by a lawyer.

"Why have we been called here?" Mrs. Topham demanded, addressing Mr. Drew. "Have you the audacity to claim that another will has been found?"

"I have the will here, Mrs. Topham," Carson Drew replied politely.

"It's preposterous!" Mrs. Topham stormed. "Josiah Crowley made only one will and in that he left everything to us!"

"It looks like a conspiracy to me," Ada added tartly, as she gazed coldly upon the relatives who were seated about the room.

Isabel did not speak, but tossed her head contemptuously. Richard Topham likewise did not offer a comment, but uneasily seated himself beside the lawyer who had accompanied him.

"If you will kindly be seated, Mrs. Topham, we will read the will," Mr. Drew suggested.

Reluctantly, Mrs. Topham obeyed.

"As you have probably learned by this time," Mr. Drew began, "a second will of the late Josiah Crowley has been found in a safety deposit box in a Masonville bank. The will is unusually long, and with your permission I will read only the portions which have to do with the disposal of the property."

Mr. Drew picked up several sheets of typewriting from the table, and after a moment's hesitation began to read in a clear voice:

" 'I, Josiah Crowley, do make this my last

will and testament, hereby revoking all former wills by me at any time made. I give and bequeath all my property, real and personal, as follows:

"'To my beloved friends and neighbors, Allie and Grace Horner, the sum of seventy-five thousand dollars each.'"

"Oh, I can't believe it!" Allie gasped.

"Neither can I!" Mrs. Topham snapped. "One hundred and fifty thousand dollars when they aren't even relatives. Why, that's nearly half of the estate. The will is a fraud!"

"There is no mistake," Mr. Drew told her quietly. Again he picked up the will and began to read:

"'To Abigail Rowen, in consideration of her kindness to me, the sum of seventy-five thousand dollars.'"

"Oh, I'm so glad," Grace murmured.

"Now, she'll be able to get the medical attention she needs," Allie added.

"I wish she could have been here," Nancy said quietly. "But I'll see to it that she is notified before the day is over."

"That old lady gets seventy-five thousand dollars?" Ada Topham demanded harshly. "What did she ever do for Crowley?" Angrily, she turned to her mother. "We kept him for years. And this is the pay we get!"

" 'To my nephews, Fred and William Mathews, the sum of twenty thousand dollars each,' " Mr. Drew read.

"We didn't expect that much," the Mathews brothers declared, in genuine surprise.

" 'To my cousins, Edna and Matilda Turner, the sum of twenty thousand dollars each.' "

"Oh, how generous!" Edna murmured.

"Aren't we mentioned at all?" Mrs. Topham broke in sharply.

Mr. Drew smiled.

"Yes, you are mentioned, but perhaps not in the way you anticipate. I'm coming to that now.

" 'To Grace and Allie Horner, my household furniture now in the possession of Mrs. Richard Topham.' "

There was a gasp of surprise from everyone in the room, and Mrs. Topham half-arose from her chair. It was generally known about River Heights that the Tophams had practically confiscated Josiah Crowley's furniture at the time they induced him to make his home with them.

"How insulting!" Mrs. Topham cried. "Does Josiah Crowley dare hint that I took his furniture?"

"I'm sure I don't know what was in his mind at the time he wrote the will," Carson Drew told her, with a smile.

"Oh, we have enough without the furniture," Grace interposed quickly. "Haven't we, Allie?"

Allie nodded.

"We'll not take the household goods from you, Mrs. Topham."

Carson Drew carefully folded the document he had been reading, and after placing it in a drawer, turned to the relatives.

"That is all there is except that there is a proviso to pay all his just debts, including his funeral expenses and that what little balance is left—maybe three or four thousand dollars—goes to the Manningham Old Men's Home. Fortunately, Josiah Crowley kept his assets in a liquid state. It will not be difficult to convert the estate into cash. For that reason I should think it would be possible to draw on your inheritances at once."

"We're actually cut off without a cent?" Richard Topham asked in disbelief. His face was unusually white.

"I am afraid you are," Mr. Drew replied.

"But it can't be," Mr. Topham returned. "You don't understand. I must have the money!"

"I can't help you. I did not make the will."

"It's a conspiracy!" Ada cried bitterly. She wheeled upon Nancy, her face convulsed with anger. "You had something to do with this, Nancy Drew," she said bitterly.

"Perhaps I had," Nancy admitted pleasantly.

"We'll break the will!" Mrs. Topham announced firmly.

"Of course you may drag the matter into court if you like," Mr. Drew responded. "But I warn you it will be only a waste of your time and money. If you don't wish to accept my judgment, ask your own lawyer."

"Mr. Drew is right," the lawyer said promptly, without waiting for Mrs. Topham to question him.

"Oh, he is, is he?" Mrs. Topham retorted. "If that's all you know about law, you're discharged! We'll get another lawyer and we'll fight to the last ditch!"

With that she arose and stalked grandly from the room. Isabel and Ada followed, after bestowing a withering glance upon Nancy. Mr. Topham brought up the rear. As soon as the door had closed behind them, their lawyer arose and picked up his brief case.

"Well, I can't say I'm sorry to lose the case," he remarked to Mr. Drew, as he, too, took his leave.

At once the atmosphere became less strained. Everyone began to talk at once.

"Oh, Nancy, I can hardly believe it yet!" Allie declared happily. "The money means so much to Grace and me! And we owe it all to you, Nancy Drew! You haven't told us how you came to find the will, but I know you were responsible."

As the Horner girls and Mr. Crowley's relatives begged her for the details, Nancy Drew told of her adventure with the robbers at Moon Lake. When she had finished the story, they praised her highly for what she had done.

"We'll never be able to thank you enough," Grace said quietly. "But after the estate has been settled, we'll try to show our appreciation."

It was on the tip of Nancy's tongue to say that she did not want a reward when Mr. Drew turned the conversation into a different channel.

"The Tophams will not give up the money without a fight," he said. "My advice would be to ask the court to appoint an administrator at once."

"We all want you, I'm sure," Grace Horner declared quickly. She regarded the others questioningly.

Everyone nodded assent.

"And of course we want you to act as our lawyer," Grace added.

"I'll be glad to assist you," Mr. Drew

promised. "If the Tophams bring the matter into court, I'll give them a battle they'll never forget!"

After thanking Mr. Drew and Nancy for what they had done, the relatives at last took their departure. Allie and Grace were the last to leave. As they turned to say good-bye to Nancy, Carson Drew opened a closet and took out the Crowley clock.

"I guess this belongs to you now," he remarked, handing the clock to Allie. "It was included in Crowley's household goods."

"I don't know what we'll do with it," Allie laughed.

Presently, the Horner girls departed with the clock. On the porch they paused to whisper significantly to Nancy:

"You'll hear from us again."

After everyone had left the house, Mr. Drew turned to his daughter with a smile.

"Well, we administered the *coup de grâce* to the Tophams all right."

"Yes, wasn't it funny to watch their faces when they learned they were cut off without a cent?"

"They took it hard. It's my opinion the Tophams won't be able to hold their heads so high after this. Richard Topham looked rather sick when he left. I suspect he's desperately in need of ready cash."

"The Tophams deserved to be cut off without a cent," Nancy Drew declared. "I'm so glad everything came out right and that Allie and Grace received the bulk of the fortune."

"Yes, they are charming girls. Unless I am mistaken they intend to reward you for what you did, Nancy."

"It wouldn't surprise me. But of course I'll not take money from them. However, if they should offer me a reward, I know what I shall ask for!"

"What is that?"

"Oh, you must wait and see," and Nancy laughed mysteriously. "They haven't offered me anything yet."

Before Carson Drew could quiz her, she skipped out the side door and vanished.

CHAPTER XXV

A Reward

"I suppose you've heard about the Tophams," Carson Drew remarked to his daughter, one morning some months after the reading of the Crowley will.

"Why, no, what about them?"

"They're practically in bankruptcy. Richard Topham has been losing steadily on the stock market of late. After his failure to recover the Crowley fortune, the banks reduced his credit. He's been forced to give up his home on the avenue."

"No, really? How that must hurt Mrs. Topham and the two girls."

"Yes, it's undoubtedly a bitter pill to swallow. They are moving into a small house this week, and from now on they'll not be able to carry themselves so high."

"I hope they don't try to make any more trouble about the will," Nancy commented. "Goodness knows, they've made enough already."

The Tophams had not given up the Crowley

estate without a bitter battle. They had put forth the claim that the will Nancy had unearthed was a forged document, but they had been unable to prove their statement. The case had finally been thrown out of court.

As administrator of the estate, Carson Drew had advanced the Horner girls and Abigail Rowen a portion of their inheritance. Several weeks before, Nancy had visited Abigail and was delighted to find her in surprisingly good health. She had secured medical attention, and a trained nurse was in constant attendance.

"I believe I'll run out into the country today and visit the Horner girls," Nancy told her father. "They telephoned yesterday and asked me to come. They hinted they had something special to tell me."

"Perhaps they're going to reward you for finding the will," Mr. Drew suggested.

"Oh, it's been nearly a month since they said anything about it," Nancy returned carelessly. "By this time they've probably forgotten all about it."

After luncheon, she set off for the farmhouse in her blue roadster. It was a beautiful autumn and Nancy Drew thoroughly enjoyed the ride.

As she came within sight of the farmhouse, Nancy was astonished at the transformation which had taken place. The house had been

given a fresh coat of white paint and a bright
green roof replaced the old one. The yard was
well kept and beds of hardy plants had been
set out.

In the barnyard, many new hen houses were
going up. Perhaps the most surprising thing
was the large number of chickens in evidence.

"Welcome to the chicken farm!" Allie
Horner cried enthusiastically, as she ran from
the house to greet Nancy.

"I never saw so many chickens in all my
life," Nancy declared.

"All Leghorns too," Allie told her proudly.

By this time Grace Horner had reached the
roadster and she too gave Nancy a hearty welcome.

"Allie is in her element these days," she
laughed. "She's putting in incubators, and
from now on will raise nothing but high-grade
fowls."

"You must see everything!" Allie insisted

Nancy was piloted from one place to another.
She saw the new chicken houses which were
being built and the incubators. But the thing
which pleased her the most was the realization
that Allie and Grace were happy in their work.

"Well, I must be getting back to River
Heights," she remarked after a time.

"Oh, you can't go yet!" Allie interposed

with a quick glance at her sister. "You tell her, Grace."

"We asked you here to-day for a special reason," Grace began a trifle awkwardly. "You see, we've been thinking for a long time that we've never done a thing to show our appreciation for what you did. We've talked with the others and everyone is agreed that we should reward——"

"Oh, I don't want a reward," Nancy broke in. "I wanted to help. And, anyway, it was fun for me."

"But we wanted to do something really handsome," Allie cried in disappointment. "It doesn't seem fair not to give you a reward."

"There's one way you can reward me if you really want to," Nancy said after a little hesitation.

"How?" Allie and Grace demanded in one breath.

"Well, it may sound silly, but I would like to have the Crowley clock for my very own."

"And is that all you want?" Grace questioned in disappointment. "We'll be glad to give you a hundred clocks if you will only take them."

"Just the old Crowley clock—that's all I care for. And if you particularly want it yourself——"

"Oh, goodness, no," Grace assured her

quickly. "It doesn't keep particularly good time and we have more heirlooms now than we know what to do with. Wait a minute and I'll get it for you."

She disappeared inside the farmhouse, returning in a few minutes with the old-fashioned timepiece. She handed it to Nancy.

"You're more than welcome to it," she declared warmly, "but it isn't a reward at all."

"It's the only reward I want," Nancy replied, smiling at the two Horner girls.

"I don't see what you want with the thing," Allie commented. "It's not much to look at."

Nancy did not reply at once, but gazed meditatively at the clock. Truly, it was not handsome; but for her it had a peculiar appeal. She could not explain to Allie and Grace just why she prized it, for her feeling was something she could not put into words. Certainly she was attached to it because of its suggestion of her recent adventure.

"I wonder if I'll ever have another half so thrilling?" Nancy thought.

As she stood gazing wistfully at the old clock she could not know that before many months had passed, she would be involved in a mystery far more baffling than the one she had just solved. Her adventures, recounted in the next volume of this series, "The Hidden Staircase," were before her. Nancy Drew did not have the power of projecting herself into the future, and yet as she looked down at the time-piece, she seemed to know that exciting days were soon to come.

"I'll always prize this clock as a trophy of my first venture as a detective," she said quietly, turning to Allie and Grace. "It will serve as a pleasant reminder of a thrilling adventure—and, who knows? perhaps as a promise for the future!"

THE END

This Isn't All!

Would you like to know what became of the good friends you have made in this book?

Would you like to read other stories continuing their adventures and experiences, or other books quite as entertaining by the same author?

On the *reverse side* of the wrapper which comes with this book, you will find a wonderful list of stories which you can buy at the same store where you got this book.

Don't throw away the Wrapper

Use it as a handy catalog of the books you want some day to have. But in case you do mislay it, write to the Publishers for a complete catalog.

THE HARDY BOY'S SERIES
By FRANKLIN W. DIXON

Individual Colored Wrappers and Text Illustrations by
WALTER S. ROGERS
Every Volume Complete in Itself.

THE HARDY BOYS are sons of a celebrated American detective, and during vacations and their off time from school they help their father by hunting down clues themselves.

THE TOWER TREASURE

A dying criminal confessed that his loot had been secreted "in the tower." It remained for the Hardy Boys to make an astonishing discovery that cleared up the mystery.

THE HOUSE ON THE CLIFF

The house had been vacant and was supposed to be haunted. Mr. Hardy started to investigate—and disappeared ! An odd tale, with plenty of excitement.

THE SECRET OF THE OLD MILL

Counterfeit money was in circulation, and the limit was reached when Mrs. Hardy took some from a stranger. A tale full of thrills.

THE MISSING CHUMS

Two of the Hardy Boys' chums take a motor trip down the coast. They disappear and are almost rescued by their friends when all are captured. A thrilling story of adventure.

HUNTING FOR HIDDEN GOLD

Mr. Hardy is injured in tracing some stolen gold. A hunt by the boys leads to an abandoned mine, and there things start to happen. A western story all boys will enjoy.

THE SHORE ROAD MYSTERY

Automobiles were disappearing most mysteriously from the Shore Road. It remained for the Hardy Boys to solve the mystery.

THE SECRET OF THE CAVES

When the boys reached the caves they came unexpectedly upon a queer old hermit.

THE MYSTERY OF CABIN ISLAND

A story of queer adventures on a rockbound island.

GROSSET & DUNLAP, Publishers, NEW YORK

THE TED SCOTT FLYING STORIES
By FRANKLIN W. DIXON

**Individual Colored Wrappers and Text Illustrations by
WALTER S. ROGERS
Each Volume Complete in Itself.**

No subject has so thoroughly caught the imagination of young America as aviation. This series has been inspired by recent daring feats of the air, and is dedicated to Lindberg, Byrd, Chamberlin and other heroes of the skies.

OVER THE OCEAN TO PARIS;
or Ted Scott's daring long distance flight.

RESCUED IN THE CLOUDS;
or, Ted Scott, Hero of the Air.

OVER THE ROCKIES WITH THE AIR MAIL;
or, Ted Scott, Lost in the Wilderness,

FIRST STOP HONOLULU;
or, Ted Scott, over the Pacific.

THE SEARCH FOR THE LOST FLYERS;
or, Ted Scott, Over the West Indies.

SOUTH OF THE RIO GRANDE;
or, Ted Scott, On a Secret Mission.

ACROSS THE PACIFIC;
or, Ted Scott's Hop to Australia.

THE LONE EAGLE OF THE BORDER;
or, Ted Scott and the Diamond Smugglers.

FLYING AGAINST TIME;
or, Breaking the Ocean to Ocean Record.

OVER THE JUNGLE TRAILS;
or, Ted Scott and the Missing Explorers.

LOST AT THE SOUTH POLE;
or, Ted Scott in Blizzard Land.

GROSSET & DUNLAP, *Publishers*, NEW YORK

THE FAMOUS ROVER BOYS SERIES

By ARTHUR M. WINFIELD

(EDWARD STRATEMEYER)

Beautiful Wrappers in Full Color

No stories for boys ever published have attained the tremendous popularity of this famous series. Since the publication of the first volume, The Rover Boys at School, some years ago, over three million copies of these books have been sold. They are well written stories dealing with the Rover boys in a great many different kinds of activities and adventures. Each volume holds something of interest to every adventure loving boy.

A complete list of titles is printed on the opposite page.

FAMOUS ROVER BOYS SERIES

BY ARTHUR M. WINFIELD
(Edward Stratemeyer)

OVER THREE MILLION COPIES SOLD OF THIS SERIES.

**Uniform Style of Binding.   Colored Wrappers.
Every Volume Complete in Itself.**

THE ROVER BOYS AT SCHOOL
THE ROVER BOYS ON THE OCEAN
THE ROVER BOYS IN THE JUNGLE
THE ROVER BOYS OUT WEST
THE ROVER BOYS ON THE GREAT LAKES
THE ROVER BOYS IN THE MOUNTAINS
THE ROVER BOYS ON LAND AND SEA
THE ROVER BOYS IN CAMP
THE ROVER BOYS ON THE RIVER
THE ROVER BOYS ON THE PLAINS
THE ROVER BOYS IN SOUTHERN WATERS
THE ROVER BOYS ON THE FARM
THE ROVER BOYS ON TREASURE ISLE
THE ROVER BOYS AT COLLEGE
THE ROVER BOYS DOWN EAST
THE ROVER BOYS IN THE AIR
THE ROVER BOYS IN NEW YORK
THE ROVER BOYS IN ALASKA
THE ROVER BOYS IN BUSINESS
THE ROVER BOYS ON A TOUR
THE ROVER BOYS AT COLBY HALL
THE ROVER BOYS ON SNOWSHOE ISLAND
THE ROVER BOYS UNDER CANVAS
THE ROVER BOYS ON A HUNT
THE ROVER BOYS IN THE LAND OF LUCK
THE ROVER BOYS AT BIG HORN RANCH
THE ROVER BOYS AT BIG BEAR LAKE
THE ROVER BOYS SHIPWRECKED
THE ROVER BOYS ON SUNSET TRAIL
THE ROVER BOYS WINNING A FORTUNE

GROSSET & DUNLAP,   PUBLISHERS,   NEW YORK

THE TOM SWIFT SERIES
By VICTOR APPLETON

**Uniform Style of Binding. Individual Colored Wrappers.
Every Volume Complete in Itself.**

Every boy possesses some form of inventive genius. Tom Swift is a bright, ingenious boy and his inventions and adventures make the most interesting kind of reading.

GROSSET & DUNLAP, *Publishers*, **NEW YORK**

THE DON STURDY SERIES
By VICTOR APPLETON

Individual Colored Wrappers and Text Illustrations by
WALTER S. ROGERS
Every Volume Complete in Itself.

In company with his uncles, one a mighty hunter and the other a noted scientist, Don Sturdy travels far and wide, gaining much useful knowledge and meeting many thrilling adventures.

DON STURDY ON THE DESERT OF MYSTERY;
An engrossing tale of the Sahara Desert, of encounters with wild animals and crafty Arabs.

DON STURDY WITH THE BIG SNAKE HUNTERS;
Don's uncle, the hunter, took an order for some of the biggest snakes to be found in South America—to be delivered alive!

DON STURDY IN THE TOMBS OF GOLD;
A fascinating tale of exploration and adventure in the Valley of Kings in Egypt.

DON STURDY ACROSS THE NORTH POLE;
A great polar blizzard nearly wrecks the airship of the explorers.

DON STURDY IN THE LAND OF VOLCANOES;
An absorbing tale of adventures among the volcanoes of Alaska.

DON STURDY IN THE PORT OF LOST SHIPS;
This story is just full of exciting and fearful experiences on the sea.

DON STURDY AMONG THE GORILLAS;
A thrilling story of adventure in darkest Africa. Don is carried over a mighty waterfall into the heart of gorilla land.

DON STURDY CAPTURED BY HEAD HUNTERS;
Don and his party are wrecked in Borneo and have thrilling adventures among the head hunters.

DON STURDY IN LION LAND;
Don and his uncles organize an expedition to capture some extra large lions alive.

GROSSET & DUNLAP, *Publishers,* NEW YORK

THE RADIO BOYS SERIES

(Trademark Registered)

By ALLEN CHAPMAN

Author of the "Railroad Series," Etc.

**Individual Colored Wrappers. Illustrated.
Every Volume Complete in Itself.**

A new series for boys giving full details of radio work, both in sending and receiving—telling how small and large amateur sets can be made and operated, and how some boys got a lot of fun and adventure out of what they did. Each volume from first to last is so thoroughly fascinating, so strictly up-to-date and accurate, we feel sure all lads will peruse them with great delight.

Each volume has a Foreword by Jack Binns, the well-known radio expert.

THE RADIO BOYS' FIRST WIRELESS

THE RADIO BOYS AT OCEAN POINT

THE RADIO BOYS AT THE SENDING STATION

THE RADIO BOYS AT MOUNTAIN PASS

THE RADIO BOYS TRAILING A VOICE

THE RADIO BOYS WITH THE FOREST RANGERS

THE RADIO BOYS WITH THE ICEBERG PATROL

THE RADIO BOYS WITH THE FLOOD FIGHTERS

THE RADIO BOYS ON SIGNAL ISLAND

THE RADIO BOYS IN GOLD VALLEY

THE RADIO BOYS AIDING THE SNOWBOUND

THE RADIO BOYS ON THE PACIFIC

GROSSET & DUNLAP, *Publishers,* NEW YORK

THE BLYTHE GIRLS BOOKS

By LAURA LEE HOPE

Author of The Outdoor Girls Series

Illustrated by Thelma Gooch

The Blythe Girls, three in number, were left alone in New York City. Helen, who went in for art and music, kept the little flat uptown, while Margy, just out of business school, obtained a position as secretary and Rose, plain-spoken and business-like, took what she called a "job" in a department store. The experiences of these girls make fascinating reading—life in the great metropolis is thrilling and full of strange adventures and surprises.

GROSSET & DUNLAP *Publishers* NEW YORK

FOR HER MAJESTY—THE GIRL OF TODAY

THE POLLY BREWSTER BOOKS
By LILLIAN ELIZABETH ROY

Polly and Eleanor have many interesting adventures on their travels which take them to all corners of the globe.

POLLY OF PEBBLY PIT
POLLY AND ELEANOR
POLLY IN NEW YORK
POLLY AND HER FRIENDS
  ABROAD
POLLY'S BUSINESS VEN-
  TURE
POLLY'S SOUTHERN CRUISE

POLLY IN SOUTH
  AMERICA
POLLY IN THE SOUTH-
  WEST
POLLY IN ALASKA
POLLY IN THE ORIENT
POLLY IN EGYPT
POLLY'S NEW FRIEND

POLLY AND CAROLA

THE GIRL SCOUTS BOOKS
By LILLIAN ELIZABETH ROY

The fun of living in the woods, of learning woodcraft, of canoe trips, of venturing into the wilderness.

GIRL SCOUTS AT DANDELION CAMP
GIRL SCOUTS IN THE ADIRONDACKS
GIRL SCOUTS IN THE ROCKIES
GIRL SCOUTS IN ARIZONA AND NEW MEXICO
GIRL SCOUTS IN THE REDWOODS
GIRL SCOUTS IN THE MAGIC CITY
OIRL SCOUTS IN GLACIER PARK

THE WOODCRAFT GIRLS AT CAMP
THE WOODCRAFT GIRLS IN THE CITY
THE WOODCRAFT GIRLS CAMPING IN MAINE
THE LITTLE WOODCRAFTER'S BOOK
THE LITTLE WOODCRAFTER'S FUN ON THE FARM

GROSSET & DUNLAP,   PUBLISHERS,   NEW YORK

THE LILIAN GARIS BOOKS

Illustrated. Every volume complete in itself.

Among her "fan" letters Lilian Garis receives some flattering testimonials of her girl readers' interest in her stories. From a class of thirty comes a vote of twenty-five naming her as their favorite author. Perhaps it is the element of live mystery that Mrs. Garis always builds her stories upon, or perhaps it is because the girls easily can translate her own sincere interest in themselves from the stories. At any rate her books prosper through the changing conditions of these times, giving pleasure, satisfaction, and, incidentally, that tactful word of inspiration, so important in literature for young girls. Mrs. Garis prefers to call her books "juvenile novels" and in them romance is never lacking.

GROSSET & DUNLAP *Publishers* NEW YORK

THE OUTDOOR GIRLS SERIES

by LAURA LEE HOPE
Author of The Blythe Girls Books

Every Volume Complete in Itself.

These are the adventures of a group of bright, fun-loving, up-to-date girls who have a common bond in their fondness for outdoor life, camping, travel and adventure. There is excitement and humor in these stories and girls will find in them the kind of pleasant associations that they seek to create among their own friends and chums.

GROSSET & DUNLAP, *Publishers,* **NEW YORK**